COUNTÉE CULLEN'S
HARLEM RENAISSANCE

TO

DR. HENRY LOUIS GATES

KB

Also by Kevin Brown

Anthologies

Best American Essays 2021
The San Diego Decameron Project: Stories from the Pandemic

Biography

Romare Bearden: Artist
Malcolm X: His Life & Legacy

Music

New York Public Library African American Desk Reference

Literary Translation

Ocosingo War Diary: Voices from Chiapas

Illuminations: A Series on American Poetics

Series Editor: Jon Thompson

Illuminations focuses on the poetics and poetic practices of the contemporary moment in the USA. The series is particularly keen to promote a set of reflective works that include, but go beyond, traditional academic prose, so we take Walter Benjamin's rich, poetic essays published under the title of *Illuminations* as an example of the kind of approach we most value. Collectively, the titles published in this series aim to engage various audiences in a dialogue that will reimagine the field of contemporary American poetics. For more about the series, please visit its website at parlorpress.com/illuminations.

Books in the Series

Countée Cullen's Harlem Renaissance: A Personal History by Kevin Brown
Things Are Completely Simple: Poetry and Translation by Brian Henry
The Poet's Tomb: The Material Soul of Poetry by Martin Corless-Smith
Vestiges: Notes, Responses, and Essays 1988–2018 by Eric Pankey
Sudden Eden by Donald Revell
Prose Poetry and the City by Donna Stonecipher

COUNTÉE CULLEN'S HARLEM RENAISSANCE

A PERSONAL HISTORY

Kevin Brown

Parlor Press
Anderson, South Carolina
www.parlorpress.com

Parlor Press LLC, Anderson, South Carolina, USA
© 2024 by Kevin Brown
All rights reserved.
Printed in the United States of America on acid-free paper.
SAN: 254-8879

Library of Congress Cataloging-in-Publication Data on File

1 2 3 4 5

978-1-64317-427-3 (paperback)
978-1-64317-428-0 (pdf)
978-1-64317-429-7 (epub)

Cover image: "The Seine, c. 1902" by Henry Ossawa Tanner. Oil on canvas. Gift
of Henry Tanner Moore to the Avalon Foundation. Courtesty of the National
Gallery of Art Collection. Public domain.
Interior and cover design: David Blakesley.

Parlor Press, LLC is an independent publisher of scholarly and trade titles in print
and multimedia formats. This book is available in paper and ebook formats from
Parlor Press on the World Wide Web at https://parlorpress.com or through on-
line and brick-and-mortar bookstores. For submission information or to find out
about Parlor Press publications, write to Parlor Press, 3015 Brackenberry Drive,
Anderson, South Carolina, 29621, or email editor@parlorpress.com.

In Memory of
Duan Nimmons Brown, 1940–1972

Our forebears could not live to know us. And yet they, who are long gone, are in us, as predisposition, as burden upon our destiny, as blood that pulsates, and as gesture that rises up out of the depths of time.

— Rainer Maria Rilke, *Letters to a Young Poet*

Contents

Foreword

I'm still not ready yet.

My mother's grandmother, born Ida Mae Roberson, was the widow of Harlem Renaissance poet Countée Cullen. The University of Chicago Press published Charles Molesworth's *And Bid Him Sing: A Biography of Countée Cullen* in 2012. I'm indebted to Molesworth and many others.

I'm an essayist, not an academic or a scholar. Any narrative solution is a finite sum of answers to an infinite series of questions relating to patterns in human life. There's no such thing as a definitive biography or autobiography, only alternate takes. This essay-cycle of twenty-four interlinked pieces about recurring characters, published between 1983 and 2023, is my personal search for a usable past. I take responsibility for any discrepancy between the way things may or may not have happened and the way things are presented or distorted. Extensive references to people, places, events and organizations are fact-based. The dialogue is not invented. The only fictional character is "me."[1]

Ida Mae Roberson, c. 1930. Family photograph. © Kevin Brown.

All writing is autobiographical writing. But this book isn't an autobiography or even a memoir in essays. Some characters in this narrative

---

1. Tape recorded interviews with Ida Cullen-Cooper and many others associated with the Harlem Renaissance are documented in David Levering Lewis's "Voices from the Renaissance" from New York Special Collections, Schomburg Center for Research in Black Culture, New York Public Library, n.p.; n.d. Unsourced exchanges between my great-grandmother and myself in this text are sometimes biographical or historical information presented as dialogue rather than exposition for purely narrative reasons. Sometimes they are things which can plausibly be assumed as characteristic of the things she said habitually but for which no archival record survives. All other dialogue is quoted directly from archived correspondence, biographies, memoirs or newspaper articles unless otherwise indicated.

are outrageous even by Balzac standards. They require no embellishment. "Life," Proust says, "contains situations more interesting, more novelistic than any novel."[2] Tell a good story well, stay out of the way.

First-names or nicknames are used where appropriate because Countée, his many friends, colleagues and students were always referred to that way when I was growing up. It was as if they'd merely slipped out into the kitchen to fix themselves a snack, and were expected back any moment.

Countée Cullen, drawing by Winold Reiss, 1925. Public domain. (See Alain Leroy Locke, p. 109.)

Acknowledgments

Expanded or abridged versions of essays from this collection originally appeared in *The American Book Review*, *The Chattahoochee Review*, *Fiction International*, *The Georgia Review*, *Kirkus Reviews*, *The Nation*, *Salmagundi* and *The Threepenny Review*.

---

2. Proust, Marcel. *Swann's Way*. Lydia Davis translation. New York. Penguin Classics (2002).

I Past Imperfect

Paris Sky BNW by Ali Sabbagh. Public domain.

An illustration from Countée Cullen's *Copper Sun*
(1927) by Charles Cullen. Public domain.

1 The Wedding

Countée's life divides in two phases: the ten years before he met Ida Mae; and the ten years after. Their eventual happy-ending marriage lacked the melodrama of his fairy-tale wedding to the daughter of William Edward Burghardt Du Bois. Which was to 1920s Harlem what the wedding of Prince Charles and Lady Diana was to the 1980s.

One Christmas eve, Countée rang the bell at Du Bois' residence; asked to see the old man. His overcoat pocket contained a tiny jewel box.

Would Dr. Du Bois grant his daughter's hand in marriage?

Du Bois was non-committal. At first, he had more questions than answers. How did Countée propose to support them both in Paris for an entire year? On the $2,500 Guggenheim Fellowship Du Bois had helped him secure?[1] Father wanted only the best for his sole-surviving child without always knowing what that best might be.

On the other hand, Countée's prospects seemed bright. His second published volume of poetry, *Copper Sun*, dedicated to Yolande, was prominently reviewed in the *New York Times*. It brought "a great deal of pleasure and satisfaction"[2] to one of Countée's favorite poets, Edwin Arlington Robinson. Countée had also signed a contract for his third book, *Caroling Dusk*, an anthology containing poems by Arnaud ("Arna") Wendell Bontemps, memoirist Langston Hughes, statesman James Weldon Johnson, novelist Claude McKay, Jean Toomer and others.[3] Countée's pedigree seemed impeccable. The couple had known each other nearly five years. What could possibly go wrong?

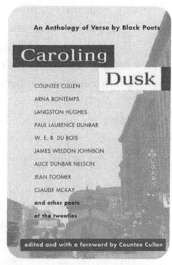

The cover of *Caroling Dusk* (1927) edited by Countée Cullen. Public domain.

1. "Guggenheim Fund Makes 75 Awards." *New York Times*, 19 March 1928, p. 8.

2. Molesworth, Charles. *And Bid Him Sing: A Biography of Countee Cullen*. Chicago: University of Chicago Press (2012), p. 125.

3. "Countée Cullen Plans Anthology," New York: *Amsterdam News*, 17 November 1926.

Du Bois warmed to the idea, but left the final decision to Yolande. Langston tried talking Countée out of it.

"Rubbish,"[4] was the reply.

Countée proposed. Yolande accepted. The couple officially engaged.

"Countée's wedding," Langston told Alain Locke, "is going to be very grand. He wants me to be an usher," Langston gushed, "with a swallow-tail coat on!"[5]

"Countée," Richard Bruce Nugent sneered, "look like one the three pigs in swallowtails."[6]

"Countée and Yolande both," Langston admitted, "are getting fat."[7]

"Fat was inevitable for Countée," Zora Neale Hurston told Langston. "It will fit him nicely too. Nice, safe, middle class."[8]

Everyone was invited, except Wallace ("Wallie") Thurman.

Wallie wore alienation like a crown. Venomous and varied, his loathing spared none, least of all himself. Not Greta Garbo, not the silky-haired, blue-veined, four-creams-and-coffee-colored black bourgeoisie (the feeling was mutual) and certainly not cops like those who busted him, his first day in New York, for indecent behavior, namely performing a sex act in a public toilet on a subway platform over the Labor Day weekend.

Wallie Thurman was many things: a hypochondriac swooning over his many ailments, real and imagined, always "near unto death."[9] But he wasn't lazy. He lived like a Bohemian, but worked like a Puritan. Sometimes, he held down two jobs, a nine-to-five

4. Letter from Countée Cullen to Harold Jackman, c. 1928, n.p.

5. Letter from Langston Hughes to Alain Locke dated 27 February 1928. New York: Alfred A. Knopf. Arnold Rampersad, David Roessel & Christa Fratantoro, eds. *Selected Letters of Langston Hughes* (2015), p. 73. https://beinecke.library.yale.edu/collections/highlights/langston-hughes-papers.

6. Nugent, Richard Bruce, quoted in Arnold Rampersad. New York: Oxford University Press. *The Life of Langston Hughes*, Vol. I (1986), p. 113.

7. Letter from Langston Hughes to Alain Locke dated 27 February 1928, *Selected Letters of Langston Hughes*, p. 73.

8. Letter from Zora Neale Hurston to Langston Hughes dated 12 April 1928. Carla Kaplan, ed. *Zora Neale Hurston: A Life in Letters* (2002), p. 19.

9. Letter from Wallace Thurman to Langston Hughes dated c. 1926. Various eds. *The Collected Writings of Wallace Thurman: A Harlem Renaissance Reader*, p. 108.

and a six-to-ten. He'd cage the occasional free meal off Paul Robeson at Craig's Restaurant. He'd bum a gin rickey or three on Irish saloon credit before midnight, when forcible ejection required several stitches above his eye. A week behind on the rent, he'd sneak into his room past his landlady. And so to bed. Passed out at 4 a.m., he'd forget to set his alarm for the day-job he was already in danger of losing, wake up at 10 a.m. not quite sober, sneak back down past the landlady, and leave for work in the freezing weather without a coat. Because he'd pawned his coat while the weather was warm.

Self-proclaimed "literary historian of the niggerati,"[10] Thurman wasn't stupid. Wallie lusted after a front-page review in the *Times Literary Supplement*, set impossibly high standards for himself, and held others to even higher ones. They never lived up to them, with notable exceptions.

Wallie described his decade-long Harlem adventure to Claude McKay thus: he "struggled and starved, and had a hell of a good time generally."[11]

"I'm not good enough," Wallie told Langston, "to be in Countée's wedding."[12]

Wallie pawned his tuxedo, and skulked off to a picturesque beach town called Santa Monica, where he could hustle up money in the Hollywood talking picture business.

"Screw 'em."[13]

*

* * *

---

10. Letter from Wallace Thurman to Langston Hughes dated c. July 1929. Various eds. *The Collected Writings of Wallace Thurman: A Harlem Renaissance Reader*, p. 120.

11. Letter from Wallace Thurman to Claude McKay dated 3 February 1928, *Collected Writings of Wallace Thurman*, p. 164.

12. Letter from Wallace Thurman to Langston Hughes dated c. early 1928, Various eds. *The Collected Writings of Wallace Thurman: A Harlem Renaissance Reader*, p. 113.

13. Letter from Wallace Thurman to Langston Hughes dated c. summer 1928. Various eds. *The Collected Writings of Wallace Thurman: A Harlem Renaissance Reader*, p. 114.

5

THE WEDDING

The most lavish African-American wedding of that social season[14] was a society-page triumph.[15] Swelling with pride, Du Bois did a mental calculus of invitees with college degrees.[16] Micro-managed every detail—right down to the engraved invitations.

Mr. and Mrs. W.E. Burghardt Du Bois
request the honor of your presence
at the marriage of their daughter Nina Yolande to Mr. Countée Cullen
on Monday, the ninth of April at six o'clock in the evening
Salem A.M.E. Church
Seventh Avenue and One Hundred Twenty Ninth Street
New York

W.E.B Du Bois c. 1911.
Public doman.

And then Du Bois had a *splendid* idea: at the conclusion of the vows, one thousand white doves would be loosed inside the church!

Countée balked. It seemed . . . well, tacky.

Nearing sixty, and at the height of his fame, the autocrat of *The Crisis*, a magazine boasting a circulation of 100,000 during "an era of rampant illiteracy, when hard labor left Afro-Americans little time or inclination for reading,"[17] W.E.B. Du Bois played an important role in the careers of many writers and visual artists.[18] As future father-in-law, Du Bois also played a complicated role in Countée's personal life. Du Bois swayed global segments of black opinion

14. "Countée Cullen Weds Daughter of Dr. Du Bois," *New York Herald Tribune*, 10 April 1928.

15. *Baltimore Sun*, 26 March 1928.

16. Historian David Levering Lewis says, "in Afro-American circles veneration of distinguished kin is practiced with an almost oriental seriousness." Lewis 233.

17. Du Bois, W.E.B. Quoted in David Levering Lewis, *W.E.B. Du Bois: Biography of a Race, 1868-1919*. New York: Henry Holt (1993).

18. At Kansas State University, Claude McKay read W.E.B. Du Bois' *The Souls of Black Folk*. He said it affected him "like an earthquake." Quoted in David Levering Lewis. New York: Alfred A. Knopf (1981); Penguin (1997). *When Harlem Was in Vogue*, p. 51.

with a mere flourish of the pen, and was famous for many things. An ability to hold his liquor was not one of them. After a nip or three, his natural abrasiveness might mellow. He might even dance. But Du Bois was habitually irascible, and bore his colossal erudition with an icy contempt people came to resent. In the face of criticism constructive or otherwise he could be reduced to outbursts of pig-headedness. He also had a knack for turning allies into enemies, was reluctant to admit mistakes, and capable of coldness toward even old friends. Papa Doc Du Bois was not to be defied.

THE CRISIS

A RECORD OF THE DARKER RACES

PUBLISHED MONTHLY BY THE NATIONAL ASSOCIATION FOR THE ADVANCEMENT OF COLORED PEOPLE, AT 70 FIFTH AVENUE, NEW YORK CITY

Conducted by
W. E. BURGHARDT DU BOIS
AUGUSTUS GRANVILLE DILL, Business Manager

Contents Copyrighted, 1915, by the National Association for the Advancement of Colored People

Contents for September, 1915

PICTURES

COVER. The Colonel of the Eighth Regiment, Ill. N. G.   Page
Thirty-nine Pictures and Portraits of Colored Chicago ....

ARTICLES

DEPARTMENTS

TEN CENTS A COPY; ONE DOLLAR A YEAR

FOREIGN SUBSCRIPTIONS TWENTY-FIVE CENTS EXTRA

RENEWALS: When a subscription blank is attached to this page a renewal of your subscription is desired. The date of the expiration of your subscription will be found on the wrapper.

CHANGE OF ADDRESS: The address of a subscriber can be changed as often as desired. In ordering a change of address, both the old and the new address must be given. Two weeks' notice is required.

MANUSCRIPTS and drawings relating to colored people are desired. They must be accompanied by return postage. If found unavailable they will be returned.

Entered as Second-class Matter in the Post Office at New York, N. Y.

The Crisis: A Record of the Darker Races (1915). Du Bois was a founding editor of the NAACP's official magazine. Public doman.

Salem African Methodist Episcopal Church was packed. Spectators arrived hours before the afternoon ceremony. Outside, an overflow crowd of 1,500, tipping their toes and craning their necks, stood on the frigid April streets in hopes of glimpsing the royal couple. Fifteen uniformed policemen, thirteen patrol officers and two sergeants, were platooned to maintain order.

Arna and Langston, in rented swallowtails and stovepipe pants, together with President Lyndon B. Johnson's future Housing and Urban Development Secretary, Robert Clifton Weaver,[19] ushered in ex-diplomat James Weldon Johnson, renaissance man of the Harlem Renaissance, along with special guests Charles S. Johnson (no relation) and Rhodes Scholar Alain Locke.

Seven more ushers and sixteen bridesmaids dressed in white Georgette gowns marched the aisles, together with 1,300 invited guests. VIPs in pews sat downstairs. Commoners gawked from the balcony.

Bridesmaids dressed in white Georgette gowns at the wedding of Countée Cullen and Yolande Du Bois, daughter of W.E.B. Du Bois in 1928 at the Salem Methodist Church. Public domain.

At 1645 hundred hours colored people's time, the Right Reverend Dr. Frederick Asbury Cullen (AB, STM, DD) presided. The bride entered on the arm of W.E.B. Du Bois (Harvard, AB 1890; Harvard, PhD 1895). An organist played the "Wedding March" from Wagner's *Lohengrin*. Countée (Harvard, AM 1926) and Yolande (Fisk University) knelt on white satin pillows. Vows were exchanged. They were pro-

19. Robert Clifton Weaver was Lyndon B. Johnson's HUD Secretary from 1966 to 1968. Weaver was the first African-American to hold a Cabinet-level position.

nounced man and wife. Countée kissed his bride. A flock of doves was loosed inside the church.

The marriage, Countée's best man Harold Jackman sneered predictively, would not last two months.[20]

20. Lewis, David Levering. New York: Alfred A. Knopf (1981); Penguin (1997). *When Harlem Was in Vogue*, p. 200.

2 Long Way from Home

Two months later Countée went to Paris, without Yolande. Arna and Langston giggled at the newspaper headline: "Groom Sails with Best Man."[1]

Countée convinces himself he has no ulterior motive other than to commence the Guggenheim fellowship DuBois had recommended him for. Countée really did have every intention of sending for Yolande once he got settled. Still, folks gossiped. It seemed, well, queer.

Countée Cullen, c. 1927, from *In Spite of Handicaps*. Public domain.

What are the unintended consequences of marrying one person and not another? Who was Ida Mae Roberson? How did they meet? What were the odds of her even marrying Countée at all? Because both were married to other people.

Ida Mae put her talent into social position and her genius into oral history. Oral history was as much a part of her character as it was Zora's. Ida Mae's tireless reminiscence, in that slight Oklahoma accent that perhaps reminded Countée of Kentucky, forms that first phase—the involuntary phase—of my immersion in Countée's life and work.

At thirty, Ida Mae left my birthplace behind: Kansas City, Missouri; ditched the man she'd married at eighteen; moved to New York City; and never looked back.[2] Ida Mae fled Jim Crow Missouri for New York to be close to her older brothers.

Orlando Roberson, whom University of California at Santa Barbara's *Discography of American Historical Recordings* credits as recording with Fats Waller in December 1929, was a popular vocalist who sang

1. Rampersad, Arnold. *The Life of Langston Hughes, Vol. 1, 1902-1941: I, Too, Sing America.* New York: Oxford University Press (1986), p. 162.

2. See, "Better to be a dishwasher in New York than head of a high school in Kansas City." Lewis 96-97.

in big bands led by Don Redman, Claude Hopkins, Edgar Hayes and Ben Selvin.[3]

Ida Mae's brother Harry Roberson, Harlem aesthete and man-about-town dabbling in acrylics and watercolors, lived to be one hundred. Like Ida Mae, Uncle Harry was a raconteur; loved lobster; and reminisced, sucking his teeth, in a cultivated variant of what George Plimpton nicknamed the Locust Valley Lockjaw. His vowwells, unaffectedly Anglicized, became plummier with each mouthful of tomalley he washed down with Harvey's Bristol Cream sherry, bright-green bits of oral history floating about in amber.

What Ida Mae learned is that "you're either up South or down South."[4]

"I came up at a time," said Ida Mae, "in Kansas City, when if you went to the theater, you sat in a certain section—Negroes upstairs. And you didn't even *go* to the theaters downtown. Back in Kansas City, where I grew up, I heard Basie play for the first time. His band had just broken up, and a fella by the name of Bennie Moten played all the local private dance clubs. He had a tonsillectomy, and died on the operating table. Meanwhile, Basie had been at Jap's Place, the colored movie house, playing organ. When Bennie Moten died, Basie took over the band. That's how Basie got his start. That's when I met Basie."[5]

Orlando Roberson, c. 1927, Public domain.

Ida Mae was born before the Black Wall Street massacre in what's known as the Greenwood Historical District of Tulsa, an oil boom-

---

3. For recordings of Orlando Roberson, see "Trees," https://www.youtube.com/watch?app=desktop&v=0bk0e4sNZ0o, and "From Our First Kiss," https://www.youtube.com/watch?v=5IVmUx3XQ5M.

4. Anderson, Annye C. with Preston Lauterbach. Foreword by Elijah Wald. *Brother Robert: Growing Up with Robert Johnson.* New York: Hachette Books (2020).

5. Lewis, David Levering. "Voices from the Renaissance."

town on the Arkansas River. Before, that region was Creek Indian territory. You could see it in her skin.

Living in New York during the 1920s, Uncle Harry and "Orlanda" were friends with Countée before she'd even met him. Her brothers formed Ida Mae's inner circle. Countée's friends Harry and Orlando overlapped that inner circle; which revolved around shared passions for card games and Broadway shows.

Countée was high-strung anyway, but also suffered from the side-effects of fame. Action items remained unacted on. Letters yellowed in their place of good intentions, unanswered. Books, unread, piled up. Invitations were very grudgingly accepted or rejected outright. Occasionally, Countée took a mental-health day, played hooky from work. But most Fridays, Countée and Uncle Harry ended the work week playing cards with friends. Which calmed Countée down.

One day Countée bumped into Uncle Harry, who insisted Countée come to his apartment. Companionable, unassuming, polite, easy to be around, Countée always tried to make others feel at ease. He tagged along. Ida Mae played a mean game of bridge. Uncle Harry needed a fourth. Countée loved food—rack of lamb, duck à l'Orange, cakes with butter cream. Ida Mae could cook. Harry introduced them.

Imagine: what must Ida Mae have felt gawking at New York for the first time? Thanks in part to redlining and other forms of segregation, in its heyday Harlem was a virtual city within the city crowding more black actors, composers, journalists, playwrights, poets, and singers into a six-square-mile radius than in all other US cities combined.[6] Riding an uptown bus, passing Central Park at 110th Street, she would have seen hordes of colored faces peering from fire escapes. As she crossed 135th Street, nine out of every ten people surrounding her would have been people of color—a quarter-million taxi drivers, businessmen, doctors, lawyers, judges, policemen—half of them African or Caribbean.

Like her brothers, Ida Mae relied on a vast national network of daily black newspapers: *The Challenger, The Chicago Defender, The Dunbar News, The Emancipator, The Messenger, The Negro World, The New York Age* and *The Pittsburgh Courier.* This network survived into the mid-1980s,

---

6. Johnson, James Weldon. *Black Manhattan.* New York: Da Capo Press (1991), p. vii.

when I reviewed *Spunk*, Zora's volume of short stories, for the *Oakland Tribune*.

Via this social network, Ida Mae could follow local and national gossip the same way myriad African-Americans beyond the Hudson did. She would have heard it through the grapevine how Zora sashayed about in dark scarves and bright turbans like some princess from India, smoking Pall Mall cigarettes, entertaining benefactors, as she scarfed down their capon and caviar, with tall-tales about her childhood chasing alligators and tomboying with lumberjacks outside Orlando.[7]

"That Zoe-rah, "Ida Mae chuckled, "she was a *mess*, child."

What would have become of Ida Mae, prisoned in Depression-era Missouri,

Cover of Zora Neale Hurston's *Spunk* (1925; 1985).

watching what Romare ("Romie") Bearden called *The Good Trains Go By* (1964), wistfully at first, then desperately, and finally in despair, as millions of others, migrants on that Illinois Central, passed her by, streaming en masse with cardboard suitcases, birdcages, old banjos, clarinets, saxophones and trap drums, in migrant trains bearing them away toward imagined-better lives in shiny Los Angeles, grimy Pittsburgh or Chicago—anywhere but here—if she herself never had managed to escape? What if she never lived to see Rome or Mexico City? Never wintered in the Caribbean light of Romie's suns? What kind of person might she have become? What might have become of me?

---

7. Langston called Zora "a perfect darkie." Langston Hughes. *The Big Sea*. New York: Knopf (1940), p. 239.

3 Countée Cullen as Himself

Who is Countée Cullen? We know much about his life, aspirations and triumphs between the ages of fifteen and forty-two: great promise shown from the time he published his first poem; many prizes won; eight or nine books published before his death. But his early life is obscured by half-truths, significant omissions and outright cover-ups.

I never got around to asking Ida Mae, before our rupture became permanent, who Countée really was deep down, or imagined himself to be. She was too proud to demand an apology. I was too proud to ask forgiveness. Then she died. It was too late.

His headstone reads, "Cullen, Countée: 1903–1946. Poet-Author-Scholar." That acute accent over the first "e" was an affectation of his teen years, not something he was born with. Nevertheless, he pronounced his name same way everybody knew him did—"Count A," not "Count T."[1]

New York City is where he was educated, and spent the majority of his short life. He deeply identified with the greater metropolitan area, a place that was home for Countée as it was for my mother and is for my only child, native New Yorkers both. Despite the fact that I'd lived there half my life at a certain point, New York City never became home for me. For me, there's no such place as home. Ida

---

1. In 1993, hearing that I was at work on a young adult biography of Cullen, Thomas Hilaire Countee, Jr., a retired attorney living in Maryland, wrote to me expressing his interest in the uncanny resemblance between his and Cullen's given name. In a privately printed genealogy of his family, he traces the roots of the name Countee or, as it sometimes appears, Conti or Contee, to the 17th century Vicomte de Conti, a Huguenot from La Rochelle, France. Emigrating to London, where his son became Lord Mayor in 1643, John and his nephew Alexander Contee, direct descendants of the Vicomte de Conti, emigrated to Charles County, Maryland, in the 18th century. The Contees prospered, settled in and around Prince George's County, acquired slaves and sired offspring. The First US Census (1790) lists three Contees in Charles and Prince George's Counties, owning nearly one-hundred slaves among them. The present Contee-Countees, black and white, are thought to derive from this branch, as the Seventh US Census (1850) lists five Maryland families bearing the surname "Countee," three of which were black.

Mae never went into detail about it except to confirm, as Langston did, that Countee [sic] Leroy Porter was in fact born in Louisville.[2]

Countée's biological father remains unknown. His birth mother appears to have given him up to his paternal grandmother, Amanda Porter, who ran a home for orphaned children in New York. When Porter died during the coldest winter anyone could remember, Countée was sent to live with local New Yorkers, his only family so far as anyone knew being distant relatives in Kentucky.

Former Detroit Urban League director John Dancy tells a story never mentioned by Ida Mae within my hearing. Working as a probation officer, he encountered Countée at the age of fifteen in a juvenile court presided over by Judge Franklin Chase Hoyt.

A youthful offender in minor trouble, Countée appeared before judge Hoyt, a descendant of US Supreme Court chief justice Samuel Chase, neatly dressed and well behaved. Judge Hoyt remanded him to Dancy's custody. Dancy and Countée rode the subway uptown to the cramped, filthy first-floor apartment room he shared with Amanda Porter, at 133rd Street between Seventh Avenue and Lenox, not far from Salem Methodist Episcopal Church. Welfare being almost non-existent at the time, Amanda Porter lived off $10 a week from the Charity Organization Society.

"He's a nice boy," Porter told Dancy, "but he doesn't have anything. He has nobody to do anything for him."[3]

It hardly matters whether Countée was conceived as a mistake brought into this world by a birth mother unable or unwilling to care for him. His birth mother reappeared in Countée's life just as he became famous, a mother Countée supported financially until 1940, the year Ida Mae married him. It matters even less whether Countée was abandoned or given up for adoption to a morbidly obese grandmother forced to take in foster children to make ends

---

2. Beulah Reimherr, a scholar who researched Countée's early years, found no trace of him either in the Louisville, Baltimore or New York City bureaus of vital statistics. Langston Hughes and Ida Mae Roberson insisted that Countée was born in Louisville. Countée himself said his poem "Ballad of the Brown Girl" was based "on an old song which every colored Kentuckian knows." Molesworth 122.

3. Perry, Margaret. Westport, Connecticut: Greenwood Press. *A Bio-Bibliography of Countee P. Cullen.* (1971), p. 106; quoting John Dancy. *Sand Against the Wind.* Detroit: Wayne State University Press (1966).

meet. It doesn't even matter whether his motive for concealing all this was image-control, insecurity over some perceived taint of illegitimacy, yearning for respectability, or all of the above. From a legal standpoint, sealing Countée's juvenile record to avoid ruining his future seems just and proper. From a writer's standpoint what matters is that, as Darryl Pinckney puts it, Countée "worked hard to conceal as much as he expressed."[4] The cumulative effect of Countée's refusal to relive painful and/or shameful experiences, of Countée's anxiousness to present only his most flattering profile to the world, up to and including stating on his resumé that he was born in New York City, would have ruined the autobiography he longed to write.

Countée's best friend Harold Jackman was one of the few Countée confided in—information perhaps Ida Mae didn't even know, or want to know. Jackman warned Countée against sharing secrets about his childhood. I'm with Jackman on this one. Half the people we tell all our troubles to can't really help; the other half don't really care. Countée seems to have taken Jackman's advice to heart. If he'd wanted the truth, the whole truth and nothing but the truth known about the years prior to his informal adoption by the Cullen family, we'd know it by now, one-hundred years after the fact.

*

What follows is the sanitized version of Countée's biography.

In *I, Too, Sing America* biographer Wil Haygood sheds light on the cultural, political, and social impact of religion on African-American life.[5] Harlem had as many as 150 black churches when Ida Mae first visited the city.[6] Vast congregations like that of Abyssinian Baptist, the platform from which Adam Clayton Powell, Jr. catapulted into Congress, were bastions of black political activism. Their pastors served as presidents of National Association for the Advance-

---

4. Pinckney, Darryl. "The Sweet Singer of Tuckahoe." *New York Review of Books* (March 5, 1992):16.

5. Haygood, Wil, ed. *I, Too, Sing America: The Harlem Renaissance at 100.* New York: Rizzoli (2018). Catalog published in conjunction with an exhibition of the same title, organized by the Columbus Museum of Art and presented 19 October 2018 through 20 January 2019 at Columbus, Ohio.

6. Johnson, James Weldon. *Black Manhattan.* New York: Da Capo Press (1991), p. 163.

ment of Colored People (NAACP) branches, collecting thousands of petition signatures in protest of racial discrimination. Such churches served as headquarters and conference centers for community outreach initiatives, establishing night schools for the illiterate and organizing voter registration drives for the disenfranchised.[7]

A deacon of Salem African Methodist Episcopal Church brought Countée's situation to the attention of the Reverend Frederick Asbury Cullen. The Reverend Cullen ran programs to steer Harlem boys away from street gangs and into artistic, athletic, educational or vocational programs. The church provided tutoring in French, Latin, math and shorthand as well as choir, orchestra and other activities.

In Maryland, the Reverend Cullen's own father had been a slave. He died when Fred was only two months old, leaving his mother to care for eleven children. Young Fred had gone about barefoot till the age of six or seven, washing his dusty feet in a ditch, wiping them dry with weeds.

Studious in the extreme, Countée attended Sunday School. The deacon considered taking Countée in himself, but knew he couldn't afford to give the boy a college education. Given the Reverend Cullen's interest in youngsters, his interest in starting his own family, the deacon asked whether Dr. Cullen would adopt the boy.

The Reverend Cullen and his wife sat Countée down for a long talk. A social worker was summoned, Kentucky relatives contacted. Countée was informally adopted by the Reverend and his wife sometime during World War I, when Countée was between the ages of eleven and fifteen, and taken to live in the fourteen-room parsonage.

Countée was an overachiever among overachievers at DeWitt Clinton High School, whose alumni include Burt Lancaster, Lionel Trilling, with whom Countée edited *The Magpie*, one of the school's two literary publications, Richard Rodgers, opera singers, painter Barnett Newman, playwright Neil Simon, and television scriptwriter Paddy Chayevsky.

---

7. Nathan Irvin Huggins says, "America's oldest 'literary' tradition, the sermon—was characteristically rhetorical, didactic oratory. But the black tradition developed its own peculiar oral tradition that extended far beyond the folk sermon. Of probably African origin was the call-and-response pattern which engaged the audience in the speaker's art." Huggins 229.

Its shelves lined with hundreds of books, Countée's third-floor study at the parsonage overlooked Seventh Avenue at 129th Street. His earliest published work is signed Countée L. Porter.[1]

Countée grew anxious to see his name on the cover of a book. By that senior year at New York University, he felt confident of enough material for a poetry collection. A published book out by September of his junior year of college, he felt, would give him a chance at winning a Rhodes Scholarship to Oxford. At twenty-two, he signed a contract with Harper & Row for a first volume of verse. When *Color* finally appeared in 1925, Robert Frost heralded Countée's emerging voice.[2] In less than a decade, he was transformed in the minds of critics and public alike from an ambitious student into one of the most celebrated black authors in the United States, a leader of the emerging Harlem Renaissance.

Countée peaked too soon, some say. He'd already reached the pinnacle of his fame.

This official version of Countée's life is what I grew up on. Failure and doubt flesh out a character as much if not more than aspirations and achievements do. In my mind, as on Ida Mae's bookshelves in Kip's Bay, Countée's life-work was an historical artifact frozen in time, not an evolutionary process. To do him justice, I needed Ida Mae to tell me what Countée was really like, not as an historical figure but as a man.

Until I'd become a working writer myself, until the challenges of sustaining creativity on a daily basis beyond middle age became real to me, I simply had no way of imagining Countée as a struggling writer: scrounging around for book-reviewing and other odd jobs, some panning out, most others not; forced to work a nine-to-five; hoping to write from six to nine; averaging at best a couple hours of off-peak work Monday through Friday, maybe three or four hours of concentrated work on Saturday and Sunday. Working writers only

---

1. Ida Mae always insisted Countée was informally adopted in or around 1914. His first published poem, written in free verse and signed Countée L. Porter, dates from 1918. See "To The Swimmer." Perry 3, citing Stanley J. Kunitz and Howard Haycraft, *Twentieth Century Authors* (New York: H.W. Wilson Co., 1942), pp. 336-337. By 1920-21, however, he began styling himself Countée P. Cullen, substantiating the theory he had been informally or otherwise adopted by the Cullens around 1918.

2. Cullen, Countée. *Color*. New York: Harper & Row (1925).

have *today*, after breakfast and before bedtime, to devote toward current and future projects. The only certainty is constant interruption, whether temporary in the form of family, financial or social obligations, or permanent in the form of death.

Ida Mae told me secrets, told me lies. She never sang me siren songs to prepare me for the hazards and temptations to come: time frittered away in well-intentioned but ultimately fruitless meetings; stressors and anxieties self-medicated with potentially lethal mixtures of nicotine, alcohol, prescription drugs or black market controlled substances; rejection slips; endless hours of research, drafting, revision and marketing on projects that ultimately go nowhere; hard-drive files irretrievably lost. She never jotted for my future reference these notes in the margins of his life. Hagiography was an open book. The rest I had to figure out for myself.

4 An Old Woman Remembers: The Harlem Renaissance

Cicely Tyson and Odetta appeared together in the made-for-television movie *The Autobiography of Ms. Jane Pittman* (1974). I close my eyes, remember Ida Mae, and picture Cicely as the one-hundred-year-old ex-slave in a chair on a front porch in Louisiana, rocking stories. This group portrait of Ida Mae and her circle couldn't be simpler than that.

Just where this redline renaissance took place is less obvious than who the major players were, what it was, when it happened or why and how it all came about.

In *I, Too Sing America: The Harlem Renaissance at 100*, Wil Haygood reminds us the Harlem Renaissance was hardly "a movement confined to either upper Manhattan or the interwar period,"[1] but was rather an "historical moment of national and international significance that continues to have reverberations far beyond its typically noted end date in the mid-1930s."[2]

If we think "Harlem" renaissance as a global movement rather than an American place, it's clear Beale Street had much in common with 125th Street. In Harlem, blues incubated at rent parties, which typically began around midnight and lasted till dawn. The cover charge was $.25, the refreshments included collard greens, bootleg liquor and jazz. Long, dark hallways abutted red-light rooms with sweaty couples bumping, grinding, slow-dancing, no dancing. Writers rubbed shoulders with blue-collar workers, numbers-runners and, of course, musicians. Duke Ellington was famous for playing rent parties. On Beale Street, or at rural juke joints deeper south, the party would "start about five o'clock and you'd go there and stay all night. You paid $.25 to get in, $.25 for a half pint of moonshine, and $.25 for a fish sandwich. Old timer told me just the other day: a "chicken sammich" wasn't nothing but a piece of Wonder bread and a piece a chicken on a platter. As long as you had some money you

---

1. Haygood, Wil. *I Too Sing America: The Harlem Renaissance at 100*. New York: Rizzoli, p. 19.
2. Ibid.

could stay all night, till the sun come up Sunday morning. They'd have one or two guys who played so you could dance."[3]

Like Memphis, Harlem was just one of many vibrant hubs in a national and international mass-communications media network—print, broadcast, graphic arts. Data routed at telegraphic speed from points Mountain West to San Francisco and Los Angeles, Chicago, Cleveland, Boston down to DC and Atlanta, over to London, Paris, Berlin and Moscow.[4]

True, most writers of this movement ended up buying one-way tickets to New York from wherever they happened to be. Zora caught the first thing smokin', and arrived in Manhattan one January with no job, no friends, $1.50 to her name and single suitcase containing a change of underwear. Rough around the edges, she was thoroughly impressed with the place.

"I hate," she told Countée, "routine."[5]

Like Arna, Wallie Thurman quit his day-job at the post office, left Los Angeles, and came to Harlem "hopefully," as Dorothy West put it, "with nothing but his nerve."[6][7] Rudolph ("Bud") Fisher arrived in New York the same year Zora and Wallie Thurman did.

True, New York in the early 1920s is where Arna, Countée and Langston began to see themselves as a group.[8] But more than a dozen of the Harlem Renaissance writers listed in Kevin Young's anthology *African American Poetry: 250 Years of Struggle & Song* were in fact born and/or raised in and around Washington, DC—Richard Bruce Nugent, Andy Razaf, Toomer, best known for that beautifully hybrid book of the Georgia plantation known as *Cane*. Others (Hughes, Hurston,

---

3. Conforth, Bruce and Gayle Dean Wardlow. *Up Jumped the Devil: The Real Life of Robert Johnson*. Chicago: Chicago Review Press (2019), p. 124.

4. Huggins, Nathan Irvin. *Harlem Renaissance*. New York: Oxford University Press, p. 56.

5. Zora Neale Hurston to Countée Cullen, 11 March 1926, quoted in Carla Kaplan, *Zora Neale Hurston: A Life in Letters* (2002), p. 84.

6. West, Dorothy. "Elephant's Dance," *Where the Wild Grape Grows, Selected Writings, 1930-1950*, p. 167.

7. Lewis, Theophilus. "Harlem Sketchbook," *Amsterdam News*, n.d.; located in Alexander Gumby papers, Special Collections, Columbia University; quoted in Steven Watson, *The Harlem Renaissance: Hub of African-American Culture, 1920-1930*. New York: Pantheon (1995), p. 85.

8. Locke, Alain. "Negro Youth Speaks," *The New Negro*, p. 47.

Locke) spent as much or more time in Washington as they did in New York. Some question whether poet Sterling A. Brown really belongs to the Harlem Renaissance at all.[9]

Ultimately, where the movement happened is less important than those who made it happen. Pre-integration, there'd been loose affiliations or siloes of black talent everywhere—as, at this so-called post-segregation writing, there still is. Suddenly, in Harlem a cadre gifted in every medium—actors, arts patrons, band leaders, composers, dancers, editors, musicians, poets, political and religious leaders ("negro preachers," Zora says, "are the first artists, the ones intelligible to the mases"),[10] set designers, theater directors, visual artists and writers from Africa, the Caribbean, North America—all emerged in just the right place at just the right time (during a flush, pre-Depression economy) to appeal to largely white audiences drunk on local color, to whom white media companies controlling the means of production had both the resources and a willingness to disseminate novel product. The balance of power, as Locke was keenly aware, remained inherently unequal.[11] But New York City had already become the principal advertising, book publishing and music recording hub of the then culturally dominant Northeast Corridor. So, this global negro renaissance came to be considered Harlem's very own.

In *The New Negro: Voices of the Harlem Renaissance*, Locke reminds us there had been, as recently as *Uncle Tom's Cabin* (1852), a literature of but not for or by the Negro. In centuries past, the black experience had been synonymous with a Negro Problem. Spokespersons, race leaders, philanthropists, sociologists and statesmen had explained us to ourselves. Now, for the first time in American history, a literature about blacks, by blacks, for blacks and anybody else who cared to listen was now a reality. The historical fact is that for black writers literary activity was a literally life-and-death undertaking. "What motivated [them] to write," says Calvin Hernton, "was the condi-

---

9. At least one historian dismisses as an historical fiction the entire concept of a Harlem "Renaissance," which presupposes there had ever been anything to be reborn. Huggins 3.

10. Letter from Zora Neale Hurston to James Weldon Johnson dated May 8, 1934, quoted in Carla Kaplan, *Zora Neale Hurston: A Life in Letters*, pp. 302-03.

11. "Aren't there," demanded H.L. Mencken impatiently on hearing that yet another worthy project had failed to find a willing white publisher, "some colored publishing firms?" Lewis 135.

tion of oppression, and what they desired of their writing was for it to ameliorate their condition."[12]

We tend to call it the black experience. But really there are only people, some of them black, most of them miscegenated to one genetically verifiable degree or other, many more of them not even realizing they're just "passing," and all of them biased in some way whether by nature or by nurture.[13] There simply is no meaningful way 1.5 billion black people scattered across Asia, Europe, South America and Oceania—to say nothing of Africa and North America—can share some universal black experience. A book like this one is, unapologetically, more about the circumstances of one African-American writer's life and family history than it is about this writer's unreliable theories about black identity.[14] Literary artists, performing artists or visual artists can't really speak for; they can only speak as.[15]

French writer Michel Leiris' training as ethnographer placed him in the impossible "position of impartial observer, detached from the system of values [one] inherits from [one's] own culture and likewise detached from the cultures [one] studies."[16] Ethnography allowed him to form "a concrete view of the social minimum that defines the human condition."[17] The essays from his collection *Brisées* are Leiris' effort to follow the many aspects of art—literary arts, performing arts, the art of translation, visual arts—as one whole in order to "ar-

---

12. Calvin Coolidge Hernton. *The Sexual Mountain and Black Women Writers*. New York: Anchor/Doubleday (1987).

13. Huggins argues that "black and white Americans have been so long and so intimately a part of one another's experience that, will it or not, they cannot be understood independently. Each has needed the other to help define himself." Huggins 11.

14. Knopf reissued James Weldon Johnson's *Autobiography of an Ex-Colored Man* in 1927. Eerily anticipating Ellison's *Invisible Man*, Johnson's hero, a frustrated musician, states: "I finally made up my mind that I would neither disclaim the black race nor claim the white race; but that I would . . . let the world take me for what it would; that it was not necessary for me to go about with a label of inferiority pasted across my forehead." *Autobiography of an Ex-Coloured Man*, p. 190.

15. Alain Locke, "Negro Youth Speaks," *The New Negro*, p. 48.

16. Leiris, Michel: *Brisées: Broken Branches*. Lydia Davis, trans., pp. 188-89.

17. *Ibid.*

rive at a complete view of man encompassing his two-fold existence as a product of culture and a fragment of nature."[18]

Seen this way, culture is perhaps best understood as a nacreous substrate peoples just naturally extrude over their experience of everyday life as they go about seeking, within natural or man-made environments, amid seemingly infinite variation, signs of unity with the unchanging One.[19]

Who contributed to the Harlem Renaissance is less disputed. There were dozens of contributors, including performing artists too numerous to mention. Old-Guard figures like Aaron ("Doug") Douglas, Du Bois, Jessie Fauset, Charles S. Johnson, James Weldon Johnson, Alain Locke, Carl ("Carlo") Van Vechten not to mention less well-intentioned mob racketeers partly dictated the tenor of the movement by sitting on jury panels, and flattering prize money out of millionaires without a clue.[20] Old Guardians like the fast-talking, night-clubbing, blond-haired, blue-eyed black man Walter White tirelessly promoted to publishers like Horace Liveright and Alfred A. Knopf next-generation writers like Owen Dodson.[21] By fits and starts, the voices of gifted and black Young Turks, both first-wave (Countée, Langston, Claude McKay) and second-wave (Arna, Zora, Bud Fisher, Bruce Nugent, Wallie Thurman and Dorothy West), were heard in the pages of the *Atlantic*, the *American Mercury*, *Crisis*, the *Dial*, the *Nation*, *Opportunity* and *Poetry*. Book contracts were entered into. The movement was in full swing.

18. *Ibid.*, 183.

19. "Langston Hughes really believed that people were producing art and culture all the time, rainbows that had to be captured before they vanished." Huggins 222.

20. Justly or otherwise, some cultural historians refer to reputedly genteel novels about "respectable" middle-class African-Americans by women of the Harlem Renaissance, Ann Lane Petry (1908-1997) in *The Street* or Jessie Redmon Fauset in *There is Confusion* (1924), *Plum Bun* (1928), *The Chinaberry Tree* (1931) and *Comedy, American Style* (1933) as the movement's "Jane Austen phase." Huggins 146. See also Lewis 274.

21. "I spoke at the Plaza last Wednesday, and devoted a good deal of time to you," future NAACP director Walter White ("Mr. N-double-ACP") told Countée, adroitly managing to steer the subject of the conversation both to its ostensible subject and to himself. "A number of the smug, fur-coated, well-fed ladies wrote down the title [of *Color*]. I hope they spend some of their money for copies." Lewis 138, 273.

Whatever you call it, wherever you locate it, the Harlem Renaissance has been written about countless times. The full story of Ida Mae's life with Countée, as it relates to History, has never yet been told.

5 Harlem Shadows

Let's not romanticize. The Harlem Renaissance was a factious social network with its fair share of back-biting, bickering, envy, grudges, long-cherished hatreds, infighting, paranoia, resentments and suspicion, reasonable and otherwise. One can hardly expect that many strong personalities to march in lock-step. Inevitably, clashes of aesthetics and politics arose among them. But there was also a lifelong sense of connection.

CLAUDE McKAY

HARLEM SHADOWS

Cover of *Harlem Shadows* by Claude McKay (1922).

McKay liked Countée as a person but didn't much care for Countée's poetry. Now Hughes! There, McKay felt, was a *real* poet. Countée and Langston had their disagreements, and much has been made of their rivalry. But Arna said that, as poets, Langston and Countée "actually had remarkably little in common."[1] If Countée's relationship with Langston was complex, Langston's relationship with Locke was Byzantine.[2] Locke's distrust of Du Bois was mutual. There was no love lost between Alain Locke and Weldon Johnson, who seemed to get along just fine with everybody else—including the cantankerous Du Bois and the quick-tempered McKay. McKay always felt like an outsider among the Talented Tenth, and didn't have much patience for pussy-footing professors like Locke. As for Charles S., fastidious and trim, outfitted in soft suits and steely spectacles, Dr. Johnson was more than happy to let Locke play the part of noisy impresario, so long as Charles S. himself wielded actual power, quietly, from behind the scenes.[3] One thing Doug, Arna, Langston and Zora could all agree on: the Harlem Renaissance would never have existed if Charles S. hadn't invented it.[4]

---

1. Perry 50, citing Arna Bontemps, "The Harlem Renaissance," *Saturday Review of Literature* 30 (22 March 1947):12.

2. Lewis 87.

3. Lewis xv.

4. Lewis 121.

Dorothy West, the movement's little sister, grew disillusioned. Even the usually irrepressible Walter White was exhausted. James Weldon Johnson's sense, on the other hand, was that though some black writers' inspiration might fail, white Southerners like Robert Penn Warren and Faulkner were illuminating the black condition with real insight.

There was still, Langston felt, some life left in the movement. He rallied Charles S. Johnson's flagging troops.

"Claude," Langston told McKay, "Countée's going to write a novel."[5]

"Darlink," he urged West, "get Doug. All the old timers aren't dead. If they're dozing, you ought to wake 'em up."[6]

Langston reassured Countée, "we are still here and strong and nobody has surpassed us."[7]

Spirituals and ragtime evolved into blues. Blues evolved into early jazz. Jazz evolved into big band swing. Swing evolved into bebop and so on into the Black Arts Movement. So, perhaps the Harlem Renaissance didn't so much flare out as continually changed venue, from turn-of-the-century gathering spots like the Marshall Hotel on West 53rd Street to the Dark Tower and other literary salons of the 1920s and 1930s to the jazz clubs, recording studios and concert halls of 52nd Street during the 1940s and 1950s.[8]

Arna Bontemps (L) and Langston Hughes. Photo courtesy of the Yale Collection of American Literature, Beinecke Rare Book and Manuscript Library, the Estates of Alberta Bontemps and Langston Hughes, and Photos by Griff Davis.

---

5. Letter from Langston Hughes to Claude McKay dated 30 September 1930, quoted in *Selected Letters of Langston Hughes*, p. 99.

6. Letter from Langston Hughes to Dorothy West dated February 22, 1934, *Where the Wild Grape Grows, Selected Writings, 1930-1950*, p. 201.

7. Letter from Langston Hughes to Countée Cullen dated 24 July 1943. *Selected Letters of Langston Hughes*, p. 252.

8. Lewis 28.

Robert Hayden's first volume of poems, *Heart-Shape in the Dust*, appeared the same year as Richard Wright's *Native Son* (1940). The Beats openly acknowledged their debt to writers like Langston and Arna. Who, as they collaborated on *Poetry of the Negro*, were in turn discovering younger novelists, poets and playwrights like Amiri Baraka, Ed Bullins, Ted Joans, Larry Neal, Ishmael Reed and Alice Walker. Ida Mae befriended younger writers like Dodson, as he went off to college. McKay returned to New York, kept in touch with Countée, and began encouraging younger visual artists like Jacob ("Jake") Lawrence. So, to a very real extent the circle remained unbroken as Romie and Jake, tutored by Augusta Savage, both had studios in the same building as McKay in the early 1940s, and continued active long after Ida Mae died.

Some say the Harlem Renaissance began as early as World War I, when McKay published e.e. cummings in *Seven Arts* literary magazine. Some say it ended as early as 1930, when Ida Mae first visited New York. Many blacks, Langston says, hadn't even "heard of the Harlem Renaissance. And if they had, it hadn't raised their wages any."[9] Most agree that, whenever it began, by the Great Depression, it was over.

Langston Hughes (1942). Farm Security
Administration photograph by Jack Delano.
Public domain.

9. Hughes, Langston. *The Big Sea*. New York: Knopf (1940), p. 228.

Prohibition was repealed before Ida Mae settled in New York. Speakeasies and night-clubs closed down. Cabarets that survived re-segregated. Harlem sang for its supper. White patrons had their fill of poontang and moonshine. The liquor wore off; the music stopped; the orgasm subsided. No longer titillated, many stopped coming to Harlem altogether.[1]

PROHIBITION ENDS AT LAST!
DECEMBER 5, 1933

"Prohibition Ends at Last" headline in the *Roaring Good Times* newspaper on December 5, 1933.

The Great Depression gripped global economies. In a pattern of reverse migration, talent fled Harlem during the late 1920s and early 1930s, returning South to Alabama, Florida, Georgia, Tennessee. Charles S. was among the first Old Guardians to leave New York. Appointed Director of Social Sciences at Fisk, he packed up his Model T, left Long Island and head-ed for Nashville. Weldon Johnson, ex-hausted, resigned from the NAACP after fourteen years of leadership. Went to Ja-pan for a year, then accepted an endowed chair in creative literature at Fisk. Living in Harlem, Du Bois said, "was a priceless experience."[2] But financial and political pressures forced him to resign from *The Crisis*, and resume his professorship at At-lanta University, where he taught history, economics, and published *Black Reconstruc-tion* (1935). Still others followed Charles S. to Nashville, where they taught till retirement.

Charles Spurgeon Johnson, c. 1940. Library of Congress, Farm Security Administration. Office of War Information Photograph Collection. Public domain.

---

1. Lewis says that c. 1926, "America was strenuously observing Prohibition by staying sempiternally and gloriously drunk." Lewis 165.

2. Du Bois, W.E.B. "The Winds of Time," *Chicago Defender*, January 1946.

For Locke, who despised the coal-dust capital of Tennessee, transferring to Fisk was simply out of the question. From Howard University, Locke watched the fad of negrophilic slumming reach a saturation point.[3]

Langston put it bluntly: "a large and enthusiastic number" of whites wasn't going to stay "crazy about Negroes" forever.[4]

Zora claimed to have seen through the negro-writer-craze from the get-go.

"Being a Negro writer these days," she told Wallie, "is a racket, and I'm going to make the most of it while it lasts."[5]

Some headed off to France or California.

Toomer disappeared into the coastal mists of Carmel, evolving, in his devotion to Gurdjieffian mysticism, toward ever higher "stages of consciousness"[6] but never again to be published by a major house.

Langston packed up his typewriter, his jazz and blues albums and the old Victrola. He shipped out third class on the *Europa*, bound for Soviet Russia.

Why?

Because, "I need," he shrugged, "the money."[7]

Zora returned to Florida to write novels, and collect folklore.

"I hate snow!"[8]

Wallie Thurman escaped, intermittently, into normalcy at Mamaroneck, Long Island, where some friends had a home, a child, and a stable marriage. There, he read and wrote, sometimes for forty-eight hours at a stretch.

---

3. A graduate of the London School of Economics, Lewis is acute on the "the politics of patronage." Lewis 178.

4. Watson 159. "Kind-hearted ofays," Huggins 131.

5. Zora Neale Hurston, quoted in Robert Hemenway, "Zora Neale Hurston and the Eatonville Anthropology." *The Harlem Renaissance Remembered*, p. 214. Huggins 131.

6. Lively, Adam. "The Talented Tenth." *London Times Literary Supplement* (30 December 1994):6.

7. Letter from Langston Hughes to Blanche Knopf dated 22 January 1934, quoted in *Selected Letters of Langston Hughes*, p. 155. Langston was cheered in the streets of Russia. Lewis 56.

8. Letter from Zora Neale Hurston to Charles S. Johnson dated 5 December 1950, quoted in Carla Kaplan, *Zora Neale Hurston: A Life in Letters* (2002), p. 633.

One week during the Christmas holidays, Dorothy West watched helpless as Wallie—against explicit doctor's orders—began drinking himself to death. He suddenly realized, eyes shocked wide open, having delirious visions of winged creatures "in the luminous void,"[9] that he was through; hemorrhaged in the charity ward at Bellevue Hospital at 2 a.m.; and died.

Wallie was thirty-two.

Thurman had savaged Countée in *Infants of the Spring*,[10] but Countée went to Wallie's funeral anyway, along with Doug, Bruce Nugent, West and Walter White. They buried him on Christmas Eve.

"He was," West eulogized, "our leader, and when he died, it all died with him."[11]

Four days later, right after Christmas, Bud Fisher died from accidental exposure to his own radiology equipment. Countée and Harold Jackman marched in that funeral procession, too.

Fisher was thirty-seven.

Classic works were composed by the half light of that movement's afterglow. *Black Manhattan* (1930), the last book James Weldon Johnson published before dying in a car crash, is rightly considered among the best histories ever written about Harlem.[12]

9. Lewis 236.

10. "[A]n obituary of the Harlem Renaissance." Huggins 191.

11. West, Dorothy. Quoted in Phyllis R. Klotman, "Wallace Henry Thurman," *Dictionary of Literary Biography*, vol. 51 (Detroit: Gale Research, 1987), p. 273.

12. Countée dubbed Weldon Johnson "the Dean of American Negro writers." Early 34.

7 The Muses Are Unemployed

As the Depression deepened, the national unemployment rate peaked at thirty-three percent. In Harlem it was almost fifty percent.[1]

Countée was broke. On Black Tuesday, he'd been in Paris during the stock market crash. Du Bois lost his home. Countée didn't receive his share of the divorce settlement. Royalty statements being few and far between, Countée was forced to continue living at home with the Reverend Cullen.

"I am making no money,"[2] he noted matter-of-factly, without rancor, living at or near the poverty level.

Countée published his novel *One Way to Heaven* (1932) the year ten thousand banks failed. President Roosevelt shut the banking system down in 1933; life savings were wiped out. Countée and twelve million other Americans were chronically unemployed. He felt financially "worse off than I've ever been before."[3]

Some writers sought relief in the Works Progress Administration. Countée had no illusions about earning a living from writing; reconciled himself to the necessity of holding down a full-time, permanent, benefitted day job his writing and lecturing income could supplement, rather than the other way around. He pounded the pavement.

Unenthused, Countée took and passed the New York City Board of Ed. teacher's exam.

"I shall teach literature if I can."[4]

Thanks in part to his connection with Weldon Johnson, Dillard University offered Countée a teaching post in New Orleans.

Everything was set: his course load, his teaching schedule. He'd packed his bags.

---

1. E. Franklin Frazier's housekeeper, having known hard times all her life, said she knew "nuthin' 'bout no depressure." Lewis 283.

2. Molesworth 177.

3. *Ibid.*

4. *Ibid.*

8 Among Schoolchildren

Countée rejected the offer because the Reverend Cullen became seriously ill.

He'd put out feelers for teaching positions at public school systems in New Jersey. Had worked as an occasional substitute at P.S. 194, but the Depression brought on a hiring freeze. The New York City Department of Education finally extended Countée a full-time offer. He began teaching French and creative writing to twelve-to-fifteen-year-olds at Public School 139, Frederick Douglass Junior High, popularly known as "139."

Increasing tension between fostering others' creative energies and nurturing his own began to take its toll. One particular student, the one who most conspicuously realized his potential, later downplayed how much, if any, Countée had actually helped him.

As faculty supervisor of the Douglass Junior High Literary Club, Countée was generous perhaps to a fault, time-wise and otherwise, in nurturing young talent. He wrote a play for his ninth-grade class, and commissioned students to write and produce theater pieces of their own. He encouraged students to write whenever possible and publish wherever possible. Countée offered constructive criticism when asked, and publication, when merited, in *The Douglass Pilot*. He recited Yeats. Or began a limerick, and prompted them to supply the last line. Once, Countée took his students on a field trip to the broadcast studio where he was to be interviewed for a radio program. He introduced the children to the listeners, and let them read their poems on air. Countée drilled students in test preparation methods, and held them to the same exacting standards he'd set for himself as he graduated, in three years instead of four, from New York University. Swiftly, many distinguished 139 alumni advanced through middle school, gained admittance to selective and even more demanding high schools like Stuyvesant or his alma mater DeWitt Clinton, continued on to Ivy League universities, and eventually became doctors, lawyers, judges, psychologists.

Teaching was no sinecure, and Countée had occasional misgivings about the profession. The days were long, the classrooms overcrowded. Dillard University had offered to have him head the English Department. As a tenured professor, he might have taught six hours per week. At 139, he taught six hours per day. Both Sam Huston [sic] College in Austin, Texas, and West Virginia State had also extended offers. Charles S. even guaranteed Countée nearly double his 139 salary to teach at Fisk and hold the Chair in Creative Literature left vacant at James Weldon Johnson's death.

Would Countée's life have been prolonged by the lighter course load, the higher pay, the greater intellectual stimulus of teaching college during his last twelve years? Probably. Would Countée have married or even met Ida Mae had he left New York during the Great Depression? Probably not.

9 James Baldwin I

One September, dressed in ragged clothes and run-over shoes, James Arthur Baldwin began his academic career at P.S. 139. Runty, effeminate of mannerism, precise in his diction, little Jimmy had trouble fitting in at first. In spite or perhaps because of his glowering intensity, he was a target for bigger boys, whom he watched furtively, with envy, and admiration. They called him "frog eyes."

What he lacked in size, he made up for in intelligence. He spent time alone at the 42nd Street library, tense, withdrawn, reading *A Tale of Two Cities*, delving into the history of Harlem. Countée, the school faculty's most widely published author, was quick to recognize, value and put to use the raw talent of his school's most gifted writing student, who'd already appeared in print by age 12.

Soon, Jimmy was contributing essays and short stories to *The Douglass Pilot*, rising to the rank of contributing editor. His final year at 139, he was named editor-in-chief.

10 Countée & Ida Mae

But by the time Yolande arrived in Paris, the marriage was already over. The rest was paperwork.

"You might as well make up your mind," Harold told Countée, "and get a divorce."[1]

Life got messy. Countée's book sales weakened. To help defray the cost of the divorce, he found himself in the embarrassing position of bumming money off his father-in-law to send Yolande home. But Du Bois' apartment had burnt down before the wedding, the expenses of which set him back one third his annual salary, and these financial distractions had forced him to swallow his enormous pride, accept a private loan equaling one year's pay. Now, at the onset of the Great Depression, the NAACP was unable to pay his wages. The great man was broke, too.[2]

A closeted man leery of betrayed confidences, when he first met Yolande, Countée confided to Locke that he'd found the solution to his problem.[3] Was Countée feeling "the pressure of social convention"?[4] Did he imagine a suitable marriage might bring him legitimacy?

As for Du Bois, how, you ask, could Harvard's first African-American PhD, patron saint of the Negro intellectuals, do anything that stupid? Let's not be too hard on him. With the notable exception of Harold Jackman, many other people seem to have bought into this charade. But a marriage does not live by the social-register alone.[5] With the benefit of nearly one hundred years' hindsight, it's clear the couple was not a good match. Yolande was an ordinary young woman trying her best to live up to the exacting standards of an extraordinary father. Both Countée, informally adopted-son of a pillar of the religious community, and Du Bois' dark princess were children

---

1. Molesworth, 138.

2. At that time, Du Bois was living at 226 W. 150th Street. He had gone nearly bankrupt paying for the wedding, which cost $5,000 in 1928 dollars, twice the median household's annual salary.

3. Quoted in Leonard Harris & Charles Molesworth, *Alain L. Locke: The Biography of a Philosopher.* Chicago: University of Chicago Press (2008), p. 160.

4. Molesworth 136.

5. "[W]hat may appear to us to be attitudes of bourgeois naiveté were often very highly race-conscious and aggressive." Huggins 6.

anxious not to disappoint. Perhaps symbolizing the collective hopes of an entire era was too much for the young couple. After eighteen months, the fairy-tale wedding officially "ended in pain, confusion, and scandalized whispers."[6]

W.E. B. DuBois with his wife Nina and daughter Nina Yolande (1901). Schomburg Center for Research in Black Culture, Photographs and Prints Division, The New York Public Library. Used by permission.

"Don't," Wallie had warned Langston, "ever marry."[7]
Langston never did.

Countée's divorce was finalized the year he met Ida Mae. He swore that if he had to continue living discreetly as a gay man "in order to preserve my health, my sanity, and my peace of mind,"[8] he would do so.

*

When they began dating, Countée would hail innumerable acquaintances with smiles and banter as he hurried Ida Mae along Lenox Avenue. Countée hated to be late, whether to a recital by the Harlem String Quartet or a concert by the Harlem Symphony. At an opera or Broadway show, that moment when the house lights dimmed, the

---

6. Molesworth 133.

7. Letter from Wallace Thurman to Langston Hughes, c. May-June 1929, *Collected Writings of Wallace Thurman*, p. 119.

8. Quoted in Leonard Harris & Charles Molesworth, *Alain L. Locke: The Biography of a Philosopher.* Chicago: University of Chicago Press (2008), p. 161.

music rose and the curtain parted was magic for him. In Ida Mae, Countée found the companionship he missed in Yolande.

In Countée, Ida Mae found somebody who broadened her horizons. She met actors, dancers, directors and musicians. Back in 1930s, she hadn't yet traveled outside the States. Mythic places Countée knew from his travels, like the Nile or River Jordan, were for Ida Mae just names from the Bible. For eleven straight years, Countée had used Paris as his base, touring Europe with friends and family—Naples, Florence, Genoa, Switzerland, Germany, Vienna; he'd twice cruised the Mediterranean by way Rome, visiting Corsica and Sicily, Alexandria and ancient Memphis; he'd toured the Middle East, seen the mosques and bazaars of Cairo, Beirut and Palestine; had made pilgrimage to the Holy Land, looked out over hills of Jerusalem, and watched the sunrise; had walked among poor Arabs along the beach at Algiers; had admired from his perch at a boarding house in the Edgware Road the vast, cool understatement of London, its gray skies punctuated by black taxis and red telephone boxes and letter boxes and double-decker buses, by royal green parks, by chimneyed vistas sprawling flat out as far as his eyes could see. Towards the end of his last year in Paris, from the Gare de Lyon as he headed south toward Marseilles, Countée began sending Ida Mae postcards. She could almost feel his thrill as his train reached the outskirts of the capital, feel the yearning he felt to live there forever.[9]

By the time I was born, Ida Mae would fly to Paris just to attend a theatrical premiere or to eat at Hayes & Gabby's soul food restaurant.

"I'm writing Ida," Arna told Langston, "today."[10]

"Ida," Langston told Arna, "tells me she is going to Paris in January for the opening of *Free and Easy*."[11]

What, Ida Mae asked Countée, was Harvard like?

"Stuffy."[12]

9. Perry 14, citing Cullen to Atkinson, 2 August 1938.

10. Letter from Arna Bontemps to Langston Hughes dated 16 December 1959. Nichols, Charles H., ed. *Arna Bontemps–Langston Hughes Letters, 1925–1967*. New York: Dodd Mead, p. 391.

11. *Ibid.*, 390.

12. Molesworth 85.

11 Physiology of a Marriage

They'd known each other ten years now.

"I know," Countée said, proposing marriage to Ida Mae, "this is right."[13]

Countée felt confident Ida Mae would be willing to overlook and understand his deficiencies, and not be too disgusted.

"Cullen Weds Ida Roberson,"[14] reads one headline. "Poet Weds Again,"[15] reads another. Chastened after a failed first marriage apiece, both decided on a ceremony as humble as Countée's royal wedding had been lavish. A few close friends gathered at the parsonage.

Scholars of LGBTQ+ studies have proved instrumental, over years of research, in helping me think this through. Countée never really left gay life. In that pre-social media era, networking was epistolary or telephonic, so the "passing of messages back and forth" must be discreet.[16] Molesworth confirms "[h]is marriage to Ida . . . did not eliminate his attraction to men, and [Countée] carefully and discretely maintained a long intimate attachment"[17] with several male lovers.

That's not to say Ida Mae was his "cover wife," window dressing in an orderly and comfortable domestic world filled with the trappings of Achievement. Most women I was raised by were strong—emasculatory, even. They never served as mere appendages of the male consort. Ida Mae was one of those who wield influence over family and community members, sometimes gently, from behind the scenes, more often not. She seemed to know what she wanted out of life; never struck me as delusional; couldn't possibly have married Countée without knowing what she was getting into.

Some things Ida Mae shared freely—promulgated. Other things she left unsaid. It's late in the historical day for "outing" Countée, even if that were my intention. But while we're on the subject of sex-

---

13. Molesworth 222.

14. *Amsterdam News*, 5 October 1940.

15. *Ibid.*

16. Molesworth 225.

17. Molesworth, pp. 207, 225. The author goes on to name, among others, dancer Edward Perry, actor Edward Atkinson, Llewellyn Ransom, Donald Duff, Ralph Loeb.

ual politics, let me with all due respect to family members who may currently administer the Countée Cullen literary estate address this particular skeleton in the closet. That way, we can move beyond rumor and innuendo and focus on what makes Countée worth writing about in the first place.

Why even bring it up? As narrator, I see Countée's self-identification somewhere along the spectrum of cisgender bisexuality, whether trending homoerotic or heteroerotic, as important to both his life and work. Being closeted seems an historical circumstance, not a character flaw. During his lifetime, he was understandably guarded about coming out. Being guarded doesn't mean he was in denial. And not being in denial doesn't mean he wasn't conflicted. How could a book-length group portrait skirt this issue?

A straight man, I spent twenty-five transformative years in San Francisco and New York. Take for granted that people span rainbows of sexual proclivity. Twice divorced, I know cohabitation with blended families and life partners is complicated. I would be naïve to think that, just because Countée had half a dozen gay lovers—apart from undocumented casual encounters—he was incapable of being a good husband. What did Ida Mae know? And when did she know it? Some might ask that. I'd rather know who managed the money. I bet she did.

Tact, discretion and old fashioned decorum dictate we don't really need to know more. But one story provides anecdotal evidence that my great grandmother's physical intimacy with her husband was not, to quote Balzac, "consummated in perfect chastity by the intervention of Death."[1]

One day, Countée and Ida Mae attended a poetry reading at the 42nd Street Library. They'd planned to spend the day in Manhattan. Sudden thundershowers developed. They hurried east to Grand Central, and took a train back to Tuckahoe. By the time it reached Westchester, Ida Mae was doubled over in abdominal pain, and could hardly walk. Countée called the doctor, who made a house call. Ida Mae had had a miscarriage. She was inconsolable.

"You can always," Countée said, assuring her they'd have a little girl next time, "try again."[2]

---

1. Balzac, Honoré de: *Lost Illusions*. Minneapolis: University of Minnesota Press. Raymond MacKenzie translation, p. xxii.

2. Molesworth 253.

In November of the year they married, Ida Mae's daughter gave birth to the first of three girls. My grandmother Norma christened my mother "Duan." As she slobbered and babbled through the years, wrapping kittens up in little red bows at Christmas while Ida Mae simmered black-eyed peas on the kitchen stove, Ida Mae played the baby grand piano, Orlando sang carols, and Uncle Harry strolled Duan about in the perambulator. Owen and others came to visit, and little Duan must have listened, slack-jawed, to Father Countée read from his works for children, *The Lost Zoo* (1940) and *My Lives and How I Lost Them* (1942).

Countée's friends became Ida Mae's, and vice versa. Some of those friendships lasted the remaining forty years of her life.

She was, Countée told her, "the best wife any man could have."[3]

I'm convinced their love for one another was genuine. Love as I understand it is a communion wherein physical attraction, mutual respect, emotional concern and intellectual compatibility may bond any two people, of any gender, to varying degrees during different phases of their relationship. Ida Mae never described anything resembling love-at-first-sight or fairy-tale romance, like an elopement in Las Vegas. It wouldn't come as any great shock for me to learn their relationship evolved to the point where she'd become more of a helpmeet to Countée than a lover. It wouldn't even surprise me if she had in fact been very comfortable with this kind of arrangement.

In *Three Guineas*, Virginia Woolf, whose relationship with Leonard Woolf serves as an example of mutually beneficial if unconventional wedlock, said that marriage is the art of choosing the human being with whom to live life successfully.[4]

Du Bois invested as much intellectual and social capital in his son-in-law's literary career as he had funds in his daughter's wedding. Was Du Bois projecting onto Countée some of the feelings of an aggrieved father whose infant son, long dead, would've been around Countée's own age? Why would Countée marry Yolande in the first place? Certainly not to get his hambone boiled. Hoping for reconciliation, at one point Du Bois had begun doing dam-

3. *Ibid.*

4. Woolf, Virginia. *Three Guineas*. New York: Harcourt Brace (1938), p. 6.

age control; tried to broker the peace. Speaking of his daughter, Du Bois had counseled Countée to "arrange to be a friend, companion and co-worker with [Yolande] and let love show itself chiefly there."[5] Countée must keep her till Christmas at least. Whatever else happened, the poet would remain welcome in the pages of Du Bois' magazine. And indeed, they continued corresponding until Countée's death. "Cullen lost a wife but retained a father-in-law."[6]

That's what Countée and Ida Mae appear to have done. What matters is that Ida Mae and Countée were good for each other, good to each other.

One thing seems clear. Neither Countée nor Ida Mae saw it coming when they first met: how they would change each other's lives; or, better yet, how successfully they would live together as their individual lives went about changing. Which may be one reason their marriage was encouraging to a young writer like Owen, despite his own same-sex orientation, and to me.

---

5. Pinckney, Darryl. "The Sweet Singer of Tuckahoe." *New York Review of Books* (March 5, 1992).

6. Watson 81.

12 The Hill & the Hollow

From the end of Prohibition, the riots of 1935, and the termination of President Franklin D. Roosevelt's vast infrastructure project, the Works Progress Administration (WPA) in 1943, Harlem declined from ghetto to slum.[1]

Countée was among the earliest of the Great Migrants to arrive, and among the last to leave. Langston always said he'd "rather have a kitchenette in Harlem than a mansion in Westchester."[2] Apart from frequent trips during which he might cross paths with Owen and others at literary functions, Langston spent the rest of his life in Harlem. As for Countée, Harlem, Ida Mae always said, was a *part* of him.

Ida Mae knew how to stretch a dollar. Until the day she died, lived as well as she could for as long as she could—in her brownstone on Riverside Drive, in that Murray Hill co-op at 10 Park Avenue, in her down-sized public-housing apartment in Kip's Bay.

Teaching public school was a living, not a killing. After they married, Countée borrowed money from rich French friends, cashed in his life insurance policy, and made the down payment on a house in Westchester. He left Harlem with a heavy heart. They took the retired Reverend Cullen along, and moved into a spacious home in Tuckahoe,[3] a one-square-mile village of streets off the central square, amid old slave plantations, just north of Bronxville and half an hour from Grand Central—just far enough outside the city to be peaceful yet close enough to be within easy commuting distance.

Boarding the train for Grand Central, Countée headed south past Fleetwood, Mount Vernon, Woodlawn Cemetery, finally arriving at 125th Street, having spanned very disparate socio-economic strata—the Hill and the Hollow—within the span of thirty minutes.

---

1. In 1925, James Weldon Johnson wondered—prophetically, as it turned out: "Will Harlem become merely a famous ghetto, or will it be a center of intellectual, cultural and economic forces exerting an influence throughout the world, especially upon Negro peoples?" Alain Locke, ed. "Harlem: The Culture Capital," *The New Negro*, p. 308.

2. Quoted in Arnold Rampersad, *The Life of Langston Hughes, Vol. II, 1941-1967: I Dream a World*. New York: Oxford University Press (1989), p. 146.

3. 41 Grand View Boulevard.

On Sugar Hill, Ida Mae and Countée lived for a time among an elite remnant of black doctors, dentists, lawyers and businessmen in a luxury apartment building landmarked historic by the American Institute of Architects. This canopied world of courtyards and liveried-doorman was peopled by neighbors like Paul Robeson and Walter White, and frequented by a steady stream of dignitaries, foreign and domestic.

In What Lewis calls "Jim Crow Harlem,"[4] in the Harlem River Valley known as The Hollow, some of Countée's students lived in crowded roach- and rat-infested, under-heated apartments. When lucky enough to find even menial jobs, their parents earned lower wages than whites, and paid more than half those wages to rent housing which cost a higher-income family less. A four-room apartment rented for half their monthly income. That same apartment cost the average white family a smaller percentage of a higher monthly income. Blacks paid higher prices for lower-quality groceries in the 125th Street stores that refused to hire them. Harlem rioted the year Jimmy became a middle-school student of Countée's at 139. Harlem rioted again two years before Baldwin graduated high school.

4. Lewis 219.

13 James Baldwin II

Jimmy became an editorial staffer on *The Magpie*, along with Richard Avedon, and was searching for a story. Countée had published *The Lost Zoo*, and was rumored to be at work on another. Jimmy proposed an interview.

What Countée may not have realized the day he agreed to meet in a vacant classroom at 139 was that, for Jimmy, this was more than a high school exercise.

Countée did sense that *something* was troubling Jimmy. Rumors circulated that Jimmy had strayed from the church, eventually left his father's house, and was seen more and more frequently in the Village. He began cutting some classes, hopelessly failing others. Defiant, Jimmy was determined that writing would be his escape and his revenge. Nothing and no one could stand in his way—certainly not naysayers who scoffed that it was madness at best and sinful Pride at worst for a poor black boy to harbor delusions so grand.

Why, when Jimmy was born, Mr. Cullen here had been among the most famous black poets alive. There was a time, not so long ago, when Young Turks like Langston had dreamed of doing in Harlem what critics like Edmund Wilson, poets like Marianne Moore, or visual artists like Georgia O'Keefe and Alfred Stieglitz were doing down in the Village. More recently, *Native Son* by Jimmy's hero Richard Wright, was proof it could be done.

In a real way, the interrogatories Jimmy propounded to Countée were questions of life and death. And Jimmy had so many questions. Where should he live? France, during the War, seemed out of the question. How should he support himself? But the answers Countée gave—the only ones he honestly *could* give, the only ones that, ultimately, Jimmy really needed—may not have been the ones Jimmy wanted to hear. Any more than Countée had wanted to hear from Walter White that premature publication of his first book, *Color*, might actually hurt rather than help his application for a Rhodes Scholarship.

How much money, Jimmy asked, could one make writing poems?

Countée was frank: "poetry cannot be considered a means of making a livelihood."[1]

"Why not?"[2]

"Poetry," Countée explained matter-of-factly, "is something which few people enjoy and which fewer people understand. A publishing house publishes poetry only to give the establishment tone. It never expects to make much money on the transaction. And it seldom does."[3]

"I never knew that." Jimmy seemed disillusioned. "I guess a teaching job comes in pretty handy, then."[4]

"Also, I *like* to teach."[5]

What, then, was the secret of literary success?

Countée cautioned that there *was* "no secret to success except hard work and getting something indefinable which we call the 'breaks'."[6]

The secret, Jimmy later learned the hard way, is to survive.

What should Jimmy *do*?

"I suggest three things—read and write—and wait."[7]

*

Between the 1935 riot Claude McKay described in *The Nation* and the 1943 riot twenty-four hours after Jimmy's 16th birthday, Countée's star pupil was forced to find his own way.

Countée had done all he could.

---

1. Early, Gerald, ed. *My Soul's High Song: The Collected Writings of Countée Cullen, Voice of the Harlem Renaissance.* New York: Doubleday (1991), p. 603.

2. *Ibid.*

3. *Ibid.*

4. *Ibid.*

5. *Ibid.*

6. *Ibid.*, 605.

7. *Ibid.*

14 Come Rain or Come Shine

Jimmy couldn't imagine the squalors of Countée's childhood. Jimmy was too caught up in his own. The irony of their interview probably escaped Jimmy: Countée was himself, at that very moment, hoping for something called the "breaks."

With the exception of summer vacations, during the 1940s Countée's academic-year rituals—mid-terms, spring break, finals, graduations—together with his domestic routine, made him a relatively stay-at-home writer. Unless Countée had school functions to attend, he caught the 4:20 p.m. train. Ida Mae would pick him at the station, and on the way home he'd talk about his day with the youngsters. Famished in the kitchen, Countée sometimes sat on a stool next to her, reading aloud from whatever he was working on. Occasionally, they went into the city to attend the Metropolitan Opera or a concert at Carnegie Hall. On weekends and holidays there were leaves to rake, antiques to bargain-hunt, and garden bulbs to plant.

Rarely, Countée took a mental health day, and played hooky from work. On Fridays, Countée and Uncle Harry still played cards. By June, when the oppressively humid New York summers arrived, Countée was exhausted. World War II rendered Europe off-limits to American tourists. So he took Ida Mae to Old Orchard Beach, Maine, instead of showing her Paris. There, with no teaching duties or yard work to do, Countée freed up his days for reading, writing, relaxing.

A thin line separates being famous from being widely misunderstood. "A real writer," Baldwin said, "is always shifting and changing and searching. The world has many labels for him, of which the most treacherous is the label of Success."[1] The conventional wisdom—wrong, in Molesworth's estimation—is that after Countée's brief investiture as Harlem's unofficial poet laureate he "faded into mediocrity."[2] At the time, Countée wasn't even thirty. What a writer really needs, Baldwin said, are "those few people who take oneself and one's work seriously enough to be unimpressed by the pub-

---

1. Baldwin, James. "Alas, Poor Richard." *Nobody Knows My Name*. New York: Library of America, p. 247.

2. Perry 59, citing *Poetry* 70 (July 1947):223.

lic hullabaloo surrounding the former or the uncritical solemnity which menaces the latter."[3]

What Molesworth thinks more likely is that "his outlook changed, his ambition shifted, and his work went in different directions."[4] The old cliché about there being no second acts in American lives seems especially untrue of Countée.[5] In his second phase as author— if not, strictly speaking, as poet—Countée was busier than ever. He wrote almost every day. Granted, he published more verse as an undergraduate than he did during his twelve-year teaching career. Only six poems appeared during his last decade. Countée's ambition wasn't diminished by the demands of family life and his day job, although his time and energy was. Whereas in college he'd been able to write and publish poems in lieu of academic papers; whereas, in Paris, living on a Guggenheim afforded him the brief luxury of writing full-time; during his last decade the tradeoff was between earning a steady paycheck and publishing sporadically.

He gave readings all over the country, even as he began thinking of ways to reinvent himself.[6] Wisely, he'd always worked in genres other than lyric poetry, a young man's game. He wrote a literary column for *Opportunity*. Worked on a libretto for the operatic stage. Sketched a series of radio plays that never found air time. Published, to varying degrees of critical acclaim but no commercial success, the novel *One Way to Heaven*. Countée published a verse/prose translation of Euripides' *Medea*, choruses from which Virgil Thomson set to music for a Museum of Modern Art premier.[7] Eventually collected as

3. Baldwin, James. "Alas, Poor Richard." *Nobody Knows My Name*. New York: Library of America, p. 259.

4. Molesworth 144.

5. "America has always loved precocious children and [Cullen] was the race's first honest-to-goodness [literary] child . . . star. Perhaps much of what happened to Cullen in his subsequent career might be better understood if we see him precisely in the light of being a child star, understanding as we do the inability of young gifted performers to sustain themselves over the long stretch of an adult career when the bloom and wonder of early achievement has rather lost its . . . charismatic tint." Early 20-21.

6. At a reading in Providence, at Brown University (Sayles Hall, December 1931) even lecturing to a crowd of 800 people, Countée might earn only $50. *Pittsburgh Courier*, 19 December 1931, p. 3.

7. "Seven Choruses from *The Medea of Euripides*."

The Medea and Some Poems (1935), it was the last book of verse he would live to see into print. Countée corresponded with figures like Richard Wright, whom he congratulated on the publication of *Native Son*. From the publication of her very first short story to the publication of *Dust Tracks on a Road*, he loyally stood by Zora, who'd alienated so many that some had written her off as "a talent in ruins."[8]

As for those "breaks" he and Jimmy discussed, Countée himself was plotting a way to write full-time. After years of fame and "strong notice but weak sales,"[9] Countée wasn't blockhead enough to write for mere fame or glory, much less for "his own amusement."[10] Had a mortgage to pay. He wanted to "to get at the masses,"[11] to make money. Between 1932 and 1945, *St. Louis Woman* was the project, that apart from *Medea* and the two children's books, consumed Countée's career.

Apart from the literary and visual arts, a mania for performing arts in general and theater in particular was common to Harlem writers of Countée's era, many of them published and produced playwrights. Ida Mae vividly recalled seeing Marc Connelly's *Green Pastures*, which premiered the year she first visited New York.[12] Performing artists like Josephine Baker, Charles Gilpin, Roland Hayes, Moms Mabley, Florence Mills and Ethel Waters starred in scores of all-black revues produced each year, half a dozen of them in New York alone, not to mention regional venues. Countée's entire circle got caught up in it, one way or another.

The plot thickens.

Langston asked Countée, "See any new plays lately?"[13]

When Arna's novel *God Sends Sunday* got good reviews in *The New York Times*, Countée thought he saw his big break.

---

8. Hemenway, Robert E. *Zora Neale Hurston: A Literary Biography*. Urbana: University of Illinois Press (1977), p. 345; quoted in Carla Kaplan, *Zora Neale Hurston: A Life in Letters* (2002), p. 591.

9. Molesworth 172.

10. Molesworth 91.

11. MSHS 605.

12. Sterling A. Brown thought *Green Pastures* "a miracle." Lewis 246.

13. Letter from Langston Hughes to Countée Cullen, April 1923, *Selected Letters of Langston Hughes*, p. 22.

"Arna," Countée said, "I feel you've got good material here for a Broadway play. Would you be interested?"[14]

Arna had never seriously considered theater till then, and—for reasons everyone involved came to understand only too well—was hesitant at first. But as the 1920s staggered into the 1930s, he grew discouraged with the sales and critical reception of his books.

Besides, what would Dr. Du Bois think?

Du Bois! Langston was mock-contemptuous. Who *cared* what Du Bois thought?

A bachelor with no dependents, Langston, spent parts of the 1930s in Latin America, translating Mexican fiction; or in Madrid during the Spanish Civil War, socializing with Hemingway. He could perhaps afford to gamble—or had less to lose.

"Never no telling," Langston egged Arna on, "what white folks will like!"[15]

"Negro stock is going up," said Bud Fisher, music arranger, author of the satiric novel *The Walls of Jericho*, "and everybody's buying."[16]

"White writers," Countée objected, were not "under the same obligations as we are to ourselves."[17]

"*You* are telling *me* about the theatre?"[18] Langston was getting worked up. "*¡Carajo! ¡Me cago en la puta madre del teatro!*"[19]

"Now what in the hell," Wallie asked, "does that mean?"[20]

---

14. Countée Cullen to Arna Bontemps, 1932.

15. Letter from Langston Hughes to Arna Bontemps dated December 9, 1966, *Selected Letters of Langston Hughes*, p. 413.

16. Hemenway, Robert E. *Zora Neale Hurston: A Literary Biography* (Urbana: University of Illinois Press, 1977), p. 345; quoted in *Zora Neale Hurston: A Life in Letters*, p. 25.

17. Huggins 293. Some think Huggins' anti-elitism seems very much of its time and place, namely the 1960s counterculture, "disillusioned by the spiritual emptiness at the top of the upward-mobility escalator," Huggins 6.

18. Letter from Langston Hughes to Arna Bontemps dated November 14, 1945, *Selected Letters of Langston Hughes*, p. 266.

19. Letter from Langston Hughes to Arna Bontemps dated 16 September 1939, *Arna Bontemps-Langston Hughes Letters*, p. 39.

20. Letter from Wallace Thurman to Langston Hughes, dated c. 1926, *Collected Writings of Wallace Thurman*, p. 109.

"Man," Langston told Countée, "in *this* or any other nation, theatre is nothing but *worriation!*"[21]

"Can't you hear," Wallie groaned, "the darkies preach."[22]

Arna still had his doubts. Against his better judgment, Arna said yes.

The scheme these three stooges hatched, a Broadway musical that eventually became *St. Louis Woman*, consumed the final twelve years of Countée's life.

They agreed to split the royalties in the event a production was staged, filmed or produced on radio. Langston did his best to help Arna and Countée get *St. Louis Woman* staged, and even helped rewrite the script.

It was frantic.

*

Right from the start, the scheme was jinxed. Orson Welles optioned *God Sends Sunday* for The Federal Theater Project. Its New York wing went dark. A production date was set out West; the Los Angeles wing folded. Same story in Chicago. Eventually, *St. Louis Woman* was produced in Cleveland.

A Hollywood producer flew out, saw the stage play, fell in love with it, and became convinced he could sell the movie rights to MGM studios—on one condition: the stage play must be rewritten as a musical, the star vehicle for Lena Horne. Critics said *St. Louis Woman* wasn't really a comedy, and was flawed even as drama. Could it really be turned into a musical?

Owen knew Lena from Brooklyn. She was poet Frank Horne's niece. A famous designer was hired to create her costumes, samples of which Countée excitedly brought home for Ida Mae to see. *St. Louis Woman*, Countée told Ida Mae, was a sure bet.

There were other problems. Although NAACP director Walter White had championed twenty years earlier the sympathetic portrayals of prostitutes in Countée's poems like "Black Magdalenes" and "The Street Called Crooked," the NAACP now protested that the

21. Langston Hughes to Arna Bontemps, *Arna Bontemps–Langston Hughes Letters, 1925-1967*, p. 180-81.

22. Letter from Wallace Thurman to Langston Hughes, dated [July 10, 1934], *Collected Writings of Wallace Thurman*, p. 130.

loose women, domestic violence and murder portrayed in *St. Louis Woman* pandered to white stereotypes of black culture, and would set the cause back one hundred years.[23]

What did Du Bois think?

He accused *God Sends Sunday* of being decadent and sordid.

"Huh?" Langston asked Arna, incredulous.[24]

"Yeah, man."[25]

"It do not," insisted Langston, "make sense."[26]

"I wholly disagree with the argument," said Walter White, "that because plays like *Porgy and Bess* have appeared on the stage, a play like *St. Louis Woman*, written by two Negroes, is justified."[27]

Owen's attempts to dissuade Lena Horne from caving to cultural politics failed. She turned down the lead role in *St. Louis Woman*; had no intention of playing a flashy lady of easy virtue.

Countée, who'd himself viewed with skepticism the 1920s commercialization of Harlem low-life, who'd always believed that art should remain aloof from politics, was now caught up in culture-wars debates about the proper portrayal of blacks in the media, and stood accused of playing down to the very stereotypes the Harlem Renaissance was in part envisioned to eradicate from the public mind. The irony was complete.[28]

When Langston saw him at a newsstand, Countée was outraged.

---

23. The overall self-consciousness of the white middle class, some insist, tends to be even more stifling among the black middle class, who lag farther behind and have farther to fall. Hence the tension in this scene between commercial viability and racial uplift in the Harlem Renaissance: "the stereotype which defined Negroes for most Americans was the obverse of the Protestant ethic." Huggins 142.

24. Letter from Langston Hughes to Arna Bontemps dated 17 April 1943, *Selected Letters of Langston Hughes*, p. 251.

25. Letter from Arna Bontemps to Langston Hughes dated 24 September 1943, *AB-LH Letters*, p. 144.

26. Letter from Langston Hughes to Arna Bontemps, n.d., *Arna Bontemps-Langston Hughes Letters*, 1925-1967, p. 181.

27. Letter from Walter White to Countée Cullen dated 19 February 1945, quoted in MSHS 68.

28. Some accused the Old Guard of being obsessed with "race image." Huggins 227.

"If I were you-all," Langston told Arna, "I'd go on with the production and pay all this prejudgment no mind."[29]

Working in Los Angeles with the song-writing team of Harold Arlen and Johnny Mercer, Arna and Countée rewrote the script yet again during one summer vacation.

At first, Countée felt relaxed and productive, urging Ida Mae to come out for a visit. But within a month of Countée's arrival in Southern California, the Reverend Cullen fell seriously ill again, this time requiring major surgery. Ida Mae remained by the Reverend Cullen's hospital bedside for a week; then had to have surgery herself.

Countée was stressed out; stress aggravated his already high blood pressure. Between cancel-controversy, feverish rewrites, and worries about his family, Countée began experiencing hypertension headaches. He also suffered from gastro-intestinal problems, his ulcer exacerbated by a tendency to worry and a weakness for rich food. He knew he should have seen a doctor. Ida Mae and the Reverend Cullen both begged him to come home. But Countée was determined to see the project through.

Everything would be OK, Countée reassured Ida Mae. When the show went on, he said, they'd go to France and live. Countée would take a year's sabbatical. That way, he could do some more writing and get things going.

The gold rush of theatrical success eventually panned out. *St. Louis Woman* went into rehearsals in mid-January 1946, and opened March 30th on Broadway, at the Martin Beck Theater. It ran *for 113 performances*, propelling Pearl Bailey, in her Broadway debut, to eventual stardom. Rouben Mamoulian, who brought audiences *Oklahoma* and *Carousel*, directed the production, best known today for that standard of the American songbook, "Come Rain or Come Shine."

Countée never lived to see it.

Countée knew he wouldn't publish another original volume of poems during his lifetime. So, he dictated a letter to his editor at Harper & Row for Ida Mae to type. It listed nearly ninety poems, both published and unpublished, representing the work he want-

---

29. Nichols, Charles H., ed. New York: Dodd Mead. *Arna Bontemps–Langston Hughes Letters*, 1925–1967 (1980).

ed to see collected in a single volume, *On These I Stand: Collected Poems, 1925–1945.*

The entire Cullen family—Ida Mae, Countée, the Reverend Cullen, Uncle Harry, my grandmother Norma, little Duan and two-time children's-book author Christopher Cat—spent Countée's last Christmas in Tuckahoe.

15 The Funeral

"How is Countée?" Zora asked.[1]

He was worse than people imagined.

His life's work was over. Ida Mae's had just begun.

Friday afternoon, Countée threw a Christmas party for the youngsters at 139, picked up his paycheck, and came home. He was to meet with Hollywood producer Ed Gross on Saturday.

Honoring commitments was something Countée always did. But he told my great-grandmother, "Ida Mae, call Ed for me. Tell him I just don't feel up to coming today. I have this awful headache. I'll stay home over the weekend and Monday—for sure—I'll be able to come down to the city."

Ida Mae called the doctor, who urged Countée to rest. He got worse. The doctor ordered him into Sydenham Hospital on January 2. During the week he was laid up, with Ida Mae at his bedside, she must have slept restlessly if at all, torn between her powerlessness to relieve his suffering, and her anxiety about what would happen to her in the very likely event he died.

When Countée suggested she carry on his work and earn herself a little money by touring, giving lectures and readings, Ida Mae lashed out in shock.

"Are you crazy?"[2]

"Everything," Countée reassured her, "will be OK."[3]

I often wonder what Ida Mae really wanted out of life. During the years I studied her she seemed above all to want security, the kind changeability of human affection couldn't imperil. I now see she wanted something more. She wanted a legacy.

Suddenly—six years after they'd married—Countée died.

Ida Mae's first official duty was to bury Countée with some semblance of dignity.

"Hey, Arna."[4]

---

1. Letter from Zora Neale Hurston to Harold Jackman dated March 29, 1944. Quoted in Carla Kaplan, ed. *Zora Neale Hurston: A Life in Letters*, p. 498.

2. Molesworth 253.

3. Molesworth, passim.

4. Routine salutation. See *AB-LH Letters*, passim.

"Yeah, Lang."[5]

"What happened to Countée?"[6]

On Wednesday, 9 January 1946 (not, as *The New York Times* reported, 10 January), Countée died at Sydenham Hospital from kidney failure precipitated by hypertension and uremic poisoning.

He was forty-two.

*

Countée's friendship with Owen carried over to Ida Mae; lasted the rest of Owen's life. Ida Mae acquired the habit of command, and expected unquestioning obedience. Owen learned easily to comply where her wishes were concerned. Me, I learned the hard way.

Ida Mae instructed that Owen do the following: (1) come to the house in Tuckahoe to help pack up some books, manuscripts and other memorabilia; (2) publish in some periodical a poem fitting as an epitaph for Countée, a master of that form; and (3) stop by the Harlem funeral home; make sure Countée was wearing a fresh shirt for the open-casket viewing; see to it his hair was brushed and combed just the way he'd liked it.

Friday morning, one day before the funeral. Owen goes to Tuckahoe. Helps Ida Mae pack some things. Goes down to Harlem. Rangs the doorbell at the underground specialist's startlingly tacky funeral establishment. At the third-storey window appears a head dressed in huge pink curlers, its torso draped in an old bathrobe. Attendant voice hollers down.

"What you want?"[7]

Might Mr. Dodson see Mr. Cullen?

Pink curlers darts inside. Head pokes back out the window.

"He ain't ready yet."[8]

Owen's innate sense of theater convinced him it was to be a long funeral.

---

5. Routine exchange. See *AB-LH Letters*, passim.

6. Letter from Langston Hughes to Arna Bontemps dated January 14, 1946; quoted in Charles H. Nichols, ed., *Arna Bontemps-Langston Hughes Letters, 1925-1967* (New York: Dodd, Mead, 1980), p. 203.

7. Hatch, James V. *Sorrow Is the Only Faithful One: The Life of Owen Dodson*. Urbana and Chicago. University of Illinois Press (1991). See Chapter 19 of this text, "Don't Come Home Early, Child."

8. *Ibid.*

On 12 January 1946, three thousand spectators stood outside Salem African Methodist Episcopal Church, freezing in the cold.

Inside, Arna, Ida Mae, Langston, Locke, Owen, Richard Wright and some of Countée's students holding flowers aloft in tribute were in attendance. Paul Robeson, Carl Van Vechten and other honorary pallbearers carried Countée's casket to its place of viewing.

The casket opened.

People moaned and wailed.

Inside, Countée was laid out in his customary dark, three-piece suit, regimental tie and starched white collar, a Phi Beta Kappa key glittering across his vest.

Owen wanted classically-trained concert soprano Dorothy Maynor to sing. Instead, an elderly congregant croaked out a song.

People wailed and moaned.

During the viewing, someone read aloud from a telegram cabled by playwright, screenwriter and director Clifford Odets. Locke, not quite five feet tall, all in gray from his hair down to his shoes, approached the casket. Stopped. Stared a long while. Then snapped four fingers to his forehead in salute.

At long last, Ida Mae stood up and read uncharacteristically angry lines from Countée's "Dark Tower."[9,10]

> We shall not always plant while others reap
> The golden increment of bursting fruit,
> Not always countenance, abject and mute,
> That lesser men should hold their brothers cheap;
> Not everlastingly while others sleep
> Shall we beguile their limbs with mellow flute,
> Not always bend to some more subtle brute;

---

9. From *The Book of American Negro Poetry*, James Weldon Johnson. ed. New York: Harcourt, Brace and Company (1922). This poem is in the public domain.

10. Some works by this author are in the US public domain because they were published before January 1, 1928. The author died in 1946, so these works are in the public domain in countries and areas where the copyright term is the author's life plus seventy-six years or less. These works may be in the public domain in countries and areas with longer native copyright terms that apply the rule of the shorter term to foreign works. Such works include the poetry collections *Color* (1925); *The Ballad of the Brown Girl* (1927); *Copper Sun* (1927). Individual poems appearing in "From the Dark Tower," (*Fire!!* (1926)), edited by Wallace Thurman. Edited Volumes include *Caroling Dusk* (1927).

We were not made eternally to weep.
The night whose sable breast relieves the stark
White stars is no less lovely being dark,
And there are buds that cannot bloom at all
In light, but crumple, piteous, and fall;
So in the dark we hide the heart that bleeds,
And wait, and tend our agonizing seeds.[11]

For her finale, Ida Mae recited her absolute favorite among all of Countée's poems, "If You Should Go."[12]

A grave is all too weak a thing
To hold my fancy long;
I'll bear a blossom with the spring,
Or be a blackbird's song,

I think that I shall fade with ease,
Melt into earth like snow,
Be food for hungry, growing trees,
Or help the lilies blow.

And if my love should lonely walk,
Quite of my nearness fain,
I may come back to her, and talk
In liquid words of rain.[13]

The service—not including interment at Woodlawn Cemetery—lasted three hours. Attendees, politely and discreetly as they could, began ducking out. By the time they laid him to rest in the cold wet ground, a pall-bearer—Arna, Harold Jackman, Langston, Owen, one of them—damn near slipped in the mud.

I ask Ida Mae what really killed Countée.

"It was that *St. Louis Woman*, child."

---

11. *Ibid.*

12. This poem is in the public domain. Reprinted in "Poem-a-Day" on June 28, 2020 by the Academy of American Poets.

13. "On Going," from *Color*, p. 105.

II Future Continuous

Audubon Park, New Orleans,© Mr. Littlehead. Creative Commons Attribution 2.0 Generic license.

16 Executrix

Countée's work went on.

Ida Mae came into her own; took over the family business. Active in the cultural life of New York, she spent the remainder of her years traveling, giving lectures, readings. As executrix of Countée's literary estate from 1947 to 1986, she dedicated herself to promoting his posthumous career.

Shortly after Countée's funeral, Richard Wright left Greenwich Village for Paris, living the remainder of his days in exile. Ida Mae's neighbor, Ralph Ellison ("a *strange* man, child"), was writing a great American novel, *Invisible Man*.[1] Lorraine Hansberry was ten years away from becoming the first black female playwright to stage a hit on Broadway, *A Raisin in the Sun*.[2]

The Harlem Renaissance ceased to be an extant movement; but its scattered remnants remained a community.

It took her three years, but Ida Mae prevailed upon the New York Public Library to rededicate the branch off Lenox, next to the Schomburg and adjacent to what had been the original site of A'Lelia Walker's Dark Tower, as the Countee [sic] Cullen Branch, and P.S. 194, on 144th Street, was re-dedicated as the Countee Cullen [sic] School.

Ida Mae had her mind made up; paid Arna a little visit down in Nashville. He was to safeguard the remains of Countée's personal archive—books, letters, manuscripts—in the Chesnutt Collection at Fisk, where Charles S. Johnson had become its first African-American president.

A decade later, truck from Yale arrives at Langston's place to cart off hundreds of letters to and from Arna, Doug, Du Bois, Jessie Fauset, Zora, Weldon Johnson, Locke, Wallie Thurman, Toomer and Walter White. The Harlem Renaissance was now enshrined.

---

1. Ellison, Ralph. *Invisible Man*. New York: Random House (1952).

2. Hansberry, Lorraine. *A Raisin in the Sun*. Modern Library. New York, NY: Random House (1957).

17 Words in the Mourning Time

Friends, colleagues and acquaintances who in their early twenties had bought one-way tickets, and reached that "rise of dreams,"[1] New York City, starving, with a lonely dollar in their pocket, while Pig-Foot Mary hawked homesick chittlins on Lenox Avenue at 135th Street; who showed up on complete strangers' doorsteps all but unannounced, their hopeful suitcases crammed full of dreams as yet undeferred, with tatters on their knees and grins on their faces; who crashed couches, and sat stoops in Strivers' Row, gossiping and guffawing, and howled dark laughter; who prowled Jungle Alley, and heard scat-singing, bull-dagging, 400-pound cross-dressers wail gut-bucket blues in dives; who, high on reefer and bootleg liquor, danced the Charleston or Lindy Hop at the Renaissance Casino and Ballroom as revolving mirror-balls shattered multicolored glitter over gowns, white ties and tails while big bands battled for a thousand and one nights;[2] who dedicated infatuate poems to one another, and corresponded from exotic ports of call the world over; who published their first books, and slept warm between hard covers; who declaimed each other's genius at turpentine jook joints in the lower depths of Dixie; who savaged each other's looks in thinly disguised satirical novels, in magazine columns, in letters privately intended for public consumption; who lost their innocent faith in friendship, fell out with each other, and, sometimes, later reconciled; who watched helpless as one of the best minds of their generation was destroyed by gin; who aged, more or less gracefully, and put on weight together; and who now, a quarter-century later, shriveled and brown as fallen leaves from early-winter trees, marching in blank, funereal lock-step, gathered together at churches and cemeteries to bury one another. Of these I sing.

---

1. Hughes, Langston. Quoted in Steven Watson. *The Harlem Renaissance: Hub of African-American Culture, 1920-1930*. New York: Pantheon (1995).

2. Lewis 30.

"I detest funerals,"[3] Langston had told Wallie, just as the latter, blind drunk at a party, flung open the window, and threatened to jump.[4]

---

3. Letter from Langston Hughes to Wallace Thurman dated 29 July 1929, quoted in *Selected Letters of Langston Hughes*, p. 91.

4. Letter from Wallace Thurman to Langston Hughes, c. May-June 1929, *Collected Writings of Wallace Thurman*, p. 119.

18 When and Where I Enter

Countée died fourteen years before I was born. Ida Mae married Robert L. Cooper, Executive Director of the Wiltwyck School for Boys in Upstate New York. He was known for his work with boxer Floyd Patterson and other troubled kids like the one I was becoming. When I was five or six, either Arna or Langston informed the other that Bob Cooper was gravely ill. Ida Mae was widowed one last time.

Old Guardians began dying off.

Yolande died just weeks before the Christmas of 1961. Her father, distraught, buried her beside his wife at the family plot in Great Barrington, Massachusetts. Du Bois lived the remainder of his life in exile, in Ghana. The intellectual architect of Pan-Africanism read, wrote and witnessed the emancipation from former colonial powers of seventeen Sub-Saharan states.[1] Growing frail, his memo-

Jean Toomer c. 1925.
Alfred Stieglitz Collection,
Courtesy National Gallery of
Art, Washington.

ry not quite what it used to be, Du Bois lived as an honorary guest of President Kwame Nkrumah. Zhou Enlai declared his birthday a national holiday at Beijing. Moscow awarded Du Bois the Lenin Peace Prize. In his own country, the prophet was feared too radical. Du Bois renounced his American citizenship, and spent the final days of his eighty-year career surrounded by portrait busts of Marx, Lenin and Chairman Mao. Moments before Martin Luther King, Jr. delivered his "I Have a Dream" speech in that August heat, the NAACP announced to a crowd as populous as Harlem at its peak that Dr. William Edward Burghardt Du Bois had died the day before.

He was ninety-five.

---

1. In 1925, Du Bois posed the question: "will France be able to make her colonies paying industrial investments and at the same time centers for such a new birth of Negro civilization and freedom as will attach to France the mass of black folk in unswerving loyalty and will to sacrifice. Such a double possibility is today by no means clear." Alain Locke, ed. W.E.B. Du Bois, "The Negro Mind Reaches Out," *The New Negro*, p. 394.

Also in 1960, Zora and Richard Wright died. Zora ended up working as a maid for $30-a-week, living at the St. Lucie County Welfare Home, collecting folk songs, voodoo spells and folk dances. Zora Neale Hurston was buried at the Garden of Heavenly Rest, open-casket, in a pink nightgown and fuzzy slippers.

When I was in second or third grade, Toomer died. The "prose oratorio"[2] *Cane* was somehow "rediscovered." It sold all of five-hundred copies during Toomer's lifetime, but Arna admired its "fractured unities" so intensely that he archived for Fisk University Library every scrap of paper Toomer ever doodled on—fifteen cartons worth.

Langston complained he'd become an unpaid ambassador for the State Department. Entertaining authors like Wole Soyinka and Léopold Senghor at Kennedy administration White House state dinners gnawed away at Langston's writing time. But he wrote relentlessly. Until he wrote no more. After sixty years of "squeezing life," as Countée put it, "like a lemon,"[3] Langston taxied himself to a hospital, checked in with severe abdominal pains, and died two weeks later. As his body was wheeled into the crematorium, celebrants chanted from "The Negro Speaks of Rivers."

As I graduated junior high and entered high school, Arna moved on from Fisk to the University of Illinois-Chicago and finally to Yale, where he curated the James Weldon Johnson Collection. Arna never stopped publishing—books for children such as I'd been or teens such as I now was, young adult biographies and histories, adult books he and Langston collaborated on, including a biography Langston hoped would be the definitive version of Hughes' life. When I was a freshman, Arna died of a heart attack, aged seventy, while working on a short-story collection.

Master's theses and doctoral dissertations about Countée began appearing as

Arna Bontemps c. 1939. Photographed by Carl Van Vechten. Library of Congress. Public domain.

2. Lewis 64.

3. Letter from Countée Cullen to Harold Jackman dated 20 July 1923.

early as the 1950s. By the mid-1960s, most of his work was out fashion, and almost all of it out of print. Then black studies departments and programs began proliferating. By the 1980s, the Harlem Renaissance was an academic industry, with Countée and other Young Turks at the heart of it. After the publication of Calvin Coolidge Hernton's primer on black feminist literature, *Sex and Racism in America* (1965), the audience had begun to shift away from writers like Claude Brown, H. Rap Brown and Eldridge Cleaver toward books like Ntozake Shange's *For Colored Girls* or Michelle Wallace's *Black Macho*. Alice Walker published *The Color Purple*. By the mid-1990s, the ill-conceived novel I'd been writing became an aborted biography, my irrecoverably failed hard drive and backups referencing hundreds of books and articles by or about Countée and the Harlem Renaissance.

*

Duan Nimmons, 1950s. Family photograph. © Kevin Brown.

I'd like to remember my mother for more than how she died. The last time I lived with Duan, in Haight-Ashbury, was not long after the Summer of Love. Overwhelmed by her struggles with alcohol and spousal abuse, she raised me intermittently. Unable to continue, she allowed networks of extended family members to take me in.

I've never believed she just gave up on me. So I've never just given up on myself. I said Ida Mae lived as well as she could for as long as she could. She did more than that. I bounced back and forth between adoptive families, distaff and sinister; spent nights in juvenile hall and county jail. Had Ida Mae not intervened, I could very easily have become a ward of the court, raised in foster care, state or federal correctional institutions.

Duan was such a tiny, little thing—5 feet 2 inches, maybe a hundred pounds. Imagine her at that New England boarding school on the Housatonic, in the Berkshires, near Du Bois' birthplace. Duan's mother certainly couldn't afford to send her to a place like that. Ida

Mae probably couldn't afford to either. But she did. Toward the end of Ida Mae's life, I could see how New York's high cost of living and 1970s hyperinflation, eroding her annuity, sent her into panic attacks at the thought of dipping into the principal.

Imagine the disconnect between the family's genteel aspirations and their lower-middle-class means. Imagine Duan's humiliation at having to bum toothpaste off kids like David Carradine. A sympathetic schoolmate of hers told me Duan began drinking early and didn't stop often.

Mama tried. Sent me to sleep-overs at summer camp; bought me a shiny new bicycle for Christmas. (Ida Mae probably paid for those, too.) Mama tried to give me the kind of normal upbringing Ida Mae and Father Countée tried to give her in Tuckahoe.

I was twelve when it happened.[4] Sent home, wherever that was, from school in Northern California, I'd visited Ida Mae at this particular suburban house before, but had never seen her cry. Had never noticed in her such pain and rage.

"Such a beautiful girl; so intelligent. How could she do that to herself? Blow her *brains* out."

Duan was thirty-two.

*

Between my father and myself there was history but no real relationship. Except for one year on the Beatnik Grand Tour, I never lived with John Henry Brown. Don't get me wrong: there was no lack of strong, black males in this boy's life—surgeons, entrepreneurs—not all of them role models. That's why I talk about them so little: I just assumed everybody had one.

My father was singular, but didn't just appear out of nowhere. Culture wasn't something he married into. After high school, back in Kansas City, he went off to Iowa University; ran track (Big 10 Track & Field record, 1959 Iowa Hawkeyes, Iowa City,

John Henry Brown, c. 1959. Family photograph. © Kevin Brown.

4. 11 November 1972.

440 Yards, 48.1 seconds), and played football for the Hawkeyes team coach Forest Evashevski, culminating in a 1959 Rose Bowl win over Cal.

John did some writing, including poetry. Whether or to what extent he participated in the Iowa Writers' Workshop I wish I knew. He was aware of it, I'm certain. Because he told me so on one of the rare occasions we spent time together, at a North Beach café.

John asked me how much I knew or remembered about Tangier, about Ted Joans, a trumpeter, born on the 4th of July, who'd roomed with Charlie Parker, and was admired by the Beats for incorporating jazz rhythms into his verse. The period John refers to, c. 1964–1965, was when Tangier was a Moroccan post-War Berlin, governed by a patchwork foreign powers including the United States. Most inhabitants spoke Arabic, Spanish or French. It was a haven for gay men. Arab street boys cost $1, bed-bug-infested hotel rooms were $.50 a day, the food was good, and the hash was strong.

Claude McKay left Harlem before the Renaissance ended. He lived in Tangier in the early 1930s, gone completely native; went about with the red fez on; threw parties for newcomers like Paul Bowles. For $25 a month, McKay had a house, an errand-boy, a live-in native woman to do the cooking, and, for entertainment, would summon, with a clapping of his hands, an eleven-year-old girl to dance before horrified guests to the accompaniment of Moroccan music.[5]

Within a year of Bowles' arrival, McKay's lease expired, his money ran out. Tired of living hand to mouth, he left. Bowles settled in Tangier the year after Countée died. Aspiring writers like my father gathered round him. Some got stranded; couldn't or wouldn't leave. "I have never seen," said William S. Burroughs, who'd have been about fifty by the time I bummed around with my father, a poet without prospects, "so many people in one place without money."[6] For Burroughs, Tangier was a shit-hole at the edge of the world— like Tijuana.

---

5. Dr. Du Bois would not have approved. During the 1920s, McKay dubbed his inner circled "the debauched tenth." Lewis 227.

6. Morgan, Ted. *Literary Outlaw: The Life and Times of William S. Burroughs.* New York: Avon. (1988).

What do I remember, in answer my father's question, before the age of reason about a bunch of drunks hanging around Dean's Bar, Mar Chica or the Parade Bar?

Nothing!

At four or five, my memories were sensory, not literary. Tangier still tastes like coconut macaroon steeped in mint tea; looked like mud-brick baked in strong sun, like women hooded in djelabas, djebalas, whatever, like Arabic calligraphy on Moorish tile. London sounded like the Beatles' "Hard Day's Night."

Claude McKay was "an exasperating individual," Arna admitted, "sour and cantankerous."[7] But Countée was a loyal admirer, and Ida Mae kept in touch with him till almost the end. McKay's eyes kept scanning involuntarily back and forth. He could no longer read or walk normally. His face paralyzed on his left, he could only eat on the right side. Poverty made him depressed, nervous and even more than usually irritable, too frail to look for work, too proud to beg from friends. He had high blood pressure, suffered from debilitating headaches, early warning signs of the stroke he eventually succumbed to. Two years after Countée died, McKay died of congestive heart failure.

Claude McKay was fifty-seven.

San Francisco had a literary tradition before Ginsberg and Bob Kaufman arrived in the mid- to late 1950s. Langston spent time in Robert Louis Stevenson's house on Russian Hill. Robert Frost's "In Dives' Dive" influenced Sterling A. Brown. Robinson Jeffers, whom Langston visited, lived just a few hours away, in Big Sur. Potrero Hill, one of the warmer, sunnier parts of The City east of the Mission District, was where San Francisco Renaissance man Kenneth Rexroth once lived. He'd moved to the Bay Area around the time Countée met Ida Mae, and went about for the longest while in that pin-striped suit Al Capone allegedly gave Rexroth during the Depression. North Beach was to the Beats what Chicago had been to Sherwood Anderson and Carl Sandburg, or Greenwich Village to many others.[8]

7. Nichols, Charles H., ed. New York: Dodd Mead. *Arna Bontemps–Langston Hughes Letters*, 1925-1967 (1980).

8. "If only," Sherwood Anderson quipped to H.L. Mencken, Anderson "could really get inside the niggers and write about them with some intelligence." Toomer was a fan of Anderson's short-story collection, *Winesburg, Ohio*. So am I.

The San Francisco Renaissance peaked, presumably, between the time Ginsberg published *Howl* and the time that I moved to Haight-Ashbury with my mother in 1969. Some of the Beats had already moved on—to Venice Beach, to New York, to Europe. But free spirits like John Henry Brown were everywhere, like that scent of Patchouli we called hippie oil, like bongo-conga sounds in Golden Gate Park. Playing outside with friends, I caught a glimpse of my father—stoned out of his mind, walking barefoot around dog shit and broken glass. I pretended not to notice.

When I lived there during my early twenties, rent on a mother-in-law apartment in the far Richmond District of San Francisco was $250 a month—wine and gourmet meals included. A heavy IBM Selectric typewriter equipped my writing desk. French windows overlooked the garden. My recliner was surrounded by bookcases and vinyl LPs. Over a period of five years, Monday through Friday, I was able to read hundreds of books just by commuting back and forth from work on BART, buses, streetcars, trolleys and cable cars. The balance between my writing life and my social life with family, friends, colleagues and acquaintances was healthier than it is now. If Philip Lamantia was to give a reading from *Becoming Visible* at City Lights Bookstore, my friends could with no fuss at all walk right up to Lawrence Ferlinghetti, and strike up a conversation.

Kevin Brown, c. 1982. Family photograph. © Kevin Brown.

About my father: I was living on the Upper West Side when the San Francisco Coroner's Office left the message on my answering machine: I was officially an orphan. Let's forget that John Henry Brown was found in the Tenderloin "with the remains of / [his] last paycheck in [his] pocket"[9]—all those verses written but never published; or published but never collected. Let's remember John Brown the way he saw himself, not as dead Beat dad. Let's remember John Brown as Poet.

---

9. Bob Kaufman, quoted in Young, Kevin, ed. *African American Poetry: 250 Years of Struggle & Song*. New York: Library of America (2020), pp. 327–37.

John Henry Brown was about sixty-one, precisely the age I am as I craft these words.

*

My childhood and adolescence were not bookish or lonely, like Langston's. Growing up in California, I spent all my extracurricular time outdoors in nature, or playing team sports. One of our classmates at Twin Peaks Elementary went on to work in Hollywood as a production manager on *Gravity* and *Mad Max: Fury Road*. We giggled when substitute teachers called on Christopher Defaria. He sounded just like Peppermint Patty. Because he was the child actor who voiced that part in *It Was a Short Summer, Charlie Brown* (1969) and *Play It Again, Charlie Brown* (1971). Sometimes, Chris sounded like Pig-Pen. Because he also voiced that part in *A Boy Named Charlie Brown* (1969).

Like Bruce Nugent, I was a compulsive reader.[10] But I hated school. Bored, disruptive, I underperformed. The school administration had no idea what else to do with me, so the school principal El Diablo took my advice: Twin Peaks let me skip fifth grade.

I was nine. Just one more year, and I'd be off to middle school, out of El Diablo's balding hair. I'd be someone else's problem. And so I was. I managed to graduate high school. Probably, they just wanted to get rid of me.

Somehow, I got into the Columbia University School of General Studies. I flunked out. Reading H.G. Wells' *Outline of History* and Bertrand Russell's *History of Western Philosophy* cover to cover in Butler Library left no time for genes or molecules. Finally, aged forty-five, I made up my mind and graduated from an academic program headquartered at the Graduate Center at the City University of New York. In 1971, faculty and administrators who believed The City University of New York should allow highly motivated students to co-design demanding yet individualized degree programs accredited the CUNY BA Program for Unique & Interdisciplinary Studies. It was literally designed for late-bloomers like me.

10· Richard Bruce Nugent arrived in Harlem at 13, worked for Rudolph Valentino, was wooed by Alain Locke, and fell in with Langston Hughes c. 1925. Bruce Nugent was contemptuous of such patently bourgeois accessories as socks and neckties. Lewis 196.

Langston says Wallie Thurman "adored bohemianism, but thought it wrong to be a bohemian."[11] Growing up, Langston bounced around the Midwest. Zora, when her mother died, left Florida at fifteen, and bummed around down South, working odd jobs at the Congressional barbershop as a manicurist, and in musical theater troupes.

It works one of two ways. Either you bounce around so much it's no wonder you're emotionally unstable, have a history of ruptured relationships, and that unsatisfied lust for stability Zora despised in Countée as "nice, safe, middle class."[12] Or, you move about from family to family, city to city, state to state, country to country, among castes, classes, races, become adaptable and resilient, disdainful of hierarchies, and phobic about downward mobility, shared bathrooms and seedy motels.

Looking at my life as a biographical essayist would, I can't see a tidy pattern of Adverse Childhood Experiences ("ACES")—drug or alcohol abuse, witnessing domestic violence, separation/divorce, mental illness, other traumas, inflicted or self-inflicted. I do see a typical product of the late 1960s and early 1970s, an era of hard drugs and easy intercourse. William S. Burroughs' *Junky* is, to me, authentically funny—as narrative, not as lifestyle. Same goes for Jim Carroll's *Basketball Diaries*, a good description of being down and out on the Lower East Side. Like many adult children of hippies, I'm skeptical of tendencies to rhapsodize Bohemian Life.

I do respond to Tom Waits' chord-portraits, songs like "Burma Shave," "$29" or "Muriel." With great gusto, I read poems and novels by what Frank Horne calls "shattered dreamers"[13]—Charles Bukowski or Bob Kaufman—artists who've survived that lifestyle long enough to write about it. I see no future in continuing to live that way myself.

---

11. Hughes, Langston. *The Big Sea*. New York: Knopf (1940). "Harlem Literati in the Twenties." *The Langston Hughes Review*. Vol. 4, No. 1 (Spring 1985), pp. 5-8. Published By: Langston Hughes Society.

12. Letter from Zora Neale Hurston to Langston Hughes dated 12 April 1928. Carla Kaplan, ed. *Zora Neale Hurston: A Life in Letters*, p. 19.

13. Horne, Frank. "Notes Found Near a Suicide," quoted in Kevin Young, ed. *African American Poetry: 250 Years of Struggle & Song*. New York: Library of America (2020), pp. 180-189.

19 Don't Come Home Early, Child

The first time I can remember visiting New York was when Carl Van Vechten died. One visit in particular, more or less narrowed down by audio-visual impressions, stands out: Toni Morrison's *Song of Solomon* (1977), published the year I was paroled from high school, in a trade paper edition of yellow, maroon and black; actor Ruby Dee's vinyl recording on Caedmon Records of Countée's *The Lost Zoo* (1978);[1] a tattered copy of *The New York Times*, opened to the obituary of Aaron Douglas, in 1979.

Those summer days we spent together changed the dynamic of our relationship. Before this, Ida Mae had never had to take me in large doses. Nor I her. We were getting on each other's nerves.

Sick to death of hearing about Countée, about the Harlem Renaissance, I was also tired of how, with Ida Mae, every *day* seemed like Black History Month.

I was, as Claude McKay described himself, "suicidally frank."[2]

"How many times we gonna hear *that* story?"

Ida Mae slitted her eyes at me.

Said, "child, you keep that up people aren't gonna wanna be around you."

To her way of thinking, I had a lot to learn both socially and professionally. Intellectual rigor and clarity are virtues. But so is the tolerant, good-natured sharing of opinions and simple pleasures in social settings via the art of conversation. Under my present conditions of sunlight and temperature, I hope someday to mellow into a highly structured yet nuanced writer, with more complex notes. At the time, harsh and tannic as immature Bordeaux, I was in need of a little ageing. The kindest thing I can say about my adolescence is that I'm outgrowing it. When I lashed out at her, Ida Mae wouldn't spank me. But boy would she *tan my hide.*

------

1. *To Make A Poet Black: The best poems of Countee Cullen* (with Ossie Davis. Caedmon Records, 1971, TC 1400).

2. Winston, James. "Interview with Winston James, author of *Claude McKay: The Making of a Black Bolshevik.*" *Jerry Jazz Musician.* 12 October 2022. https://jerry-jazzmusician.com/interview-with-winston-james-author-of-claude-mckay-the-making-of-a-black-bolshevik/

Growing up, I saw how much pride Ida Mae took in her wide circle of friends, in her role as executrix of the Countée Cullen literary estate. Even after her eventual remarriage, she remained as faithful to Countée's memory as Queen Victoria did to Prince Albert's. In certain quarters, she commanded the kind of respect accorded the likes of Eleanor Roosevelt just for being what, in essence, Ida Mae was: activist, former first lady. From my childhood right up until her funeral, I never knew a time when she was *not* conducting affairs of estate. David Levering Lewis and other writers, tape recorders in hand, arrived to conduct oral history interviews with her. Writers from apartheid-era South Africa, from Nigeria would come pay their respects to Ida Mae, fondly remembering how first hearing Countée's poetry as children had profoundly influenced their decision to become writers themselves. She was gradually transformed into a griot woman, granting audience to newspapers and radio, fielding inquiries, receiving visits from pilgrims foreign and domestic. She became the embodiment of a living tradition.

In *African American Poetry: 250 Years of Struggle and Song*, Young introduces Dodson to a wider audience. Dodson wrote poems both experimental and traditional, "The Morning Duke Ellington Praised the Lord and Six Little Black Davids Tapped Danced Unto" and "Sorrow Is the Only Faithful One."

First Period

It was one of those 3H days in New York—hazy, hot and humid. Ida Mae took me over to the West Side to meet Owen in the 13th-floor penthouse he shared with his sister on 51st Street. Down below, yellow horns bopped cacophony through the canyons, contrapuntal.

Ida Mae had a habit that annoyed me. She would recite a distinguished friend or colleague's resume like a collector quoting an artwork's provenance.

"Owen is a novelist. He's written thirty-seven plays and operas, twenty-seven of which have been produced, two of them at Kennedy Center."

She went on and on and on about his production of Jimmy Baldwin's *Amen Corner*, of Chekhov's *Cherry Orchard*, of T.S. Eliot's *Murder in the Cathedral*, of Tennessee Williams' *The Glass Menagerie*; about how Owen won a Guggenheim Fellowship, just like Countée; about how

President Lyndon Johnson invited Owen to the White House for a celebration of Shakespeare's 400th.

I suspect Ida Mae arranged this little visit for several reasons. Not least of which was that if I were as serious about writing as I claimed to be, had anywhere near as much talent as I thought I had, then Owen would know what to make of it.

From the very beginning, Ida Mae, physically distant as she might be, played a role in shaping my life without my realizing it. She was partly responsible for keeping me alive during the years between 1960 and 1980. But, then, as Baldwin puts it, "the problems of keeping children alive are not real for children."[3]

Ida Mae bought that expensive hockey gear I wore, back when the California Golden Seals played in the National Hockey League. Hockey demands that toddlers learn to skate almost as soon as walk; leave home during their teens to live with networks of extended hockey families; sacrifice teeth and entire decades of their short careers to a game injury forces most into retirement from by the average age of twenty-eight. Ice hockey, like writing, reveres its history and tradition. Commentators talk about power forwards and lethal shots. They also talk finesse, hockey IQ, of players—the vast majority of whom did not graduate from Cornell—who are students of the game. Ida Mae ensured I got scouted by a coach used to developing raw talent.

Baldwin wrote some classic essays from *Notes of a Native Son* while living at Owen's apartment. Like a teenage prospect aspiring to the American Hockey League or the National Hockey League, I suddenly find myself in league with heavier, faster, savvier opponents who have neither the time nor inclination to take it easy on me. Owen was a decade younger than Countée. But Countée treated Owen as an equal, not a protégé. And this, I now see, is the treatment Owen was about to mete out to me, though I was still in Juniors.

Could I think on my feet? Would I prove as effective in the give-and-take of improvised conversation as on the through-composed page? Most crucially, could I *stay healthy*? Each and every failure to finish, every turnover, every blown coverage, every sloppy shift change, every battle lost along the boards, every failure to read the

---

3. Baldwin, James. "Notes of a Native Son," from *Notes of a Native Son*. Boston. Beacon Press (1955).

play as it developed would be closely scrutinized. And if I didn't perform to potential I would be cut or, if I was lucky, sent down. This was my amateur tryout.

As a writer, I've been given quality scoring chances but never coddled by veterans. Just the opposite: I'd better not be wasting their time and generosity if they went out on a limb to secure me access to an agent, magazine editor or book publisher.

There are five of us in Owen's apartment. Ida Mae does the play-by-play.

"That's Edith, Owen's sister."

Edith doesn't say much, but does do some officiating; drops the face-off puck.

"Child," Ida Mae gestures toward a regular seated across the dining room table, "I'd like you to meet Noel Da Costa—classical violinist, conductor, jazz composer. He teaches over there at Rutgers, don't you know."[4]

I sense these are connoisseurs of performance. Today's not a good day for a bad game. But I must learn not to panic with the puck, under pressure. To my surprise, I find that the higher the stakes the better I feel. If I do have any pre-game jitters, there's no time to dwell on them.

I shake Noel's hand.

"You were one of Countée's students, I understand."

"Mmm hmm."

You can tell Ida Mae's at ease because she spits her mouthpiece out into her glove.[5]

"Hush yo' mouf, child!"

---

4. See https://en.wikipedia.org/wiki/Noel_DaCosta.

5. Wikipedia defines "creative nonfiction (also known as literary nonfiction or narrative nonfiction or literary journalism or verfabula) as a genre of writing that uses [novelistic] techniques to create factually accurate narratives. Creative nonfiction contrasts with other nonfiction, such as academic or technical writing or journalism, which are also rooted in accurate fact though not written to entertain based on prose style. Many writers view creative nonfiction as overlapping with the essay." https://en.wikipedia.org/wiki/Creative_nonfiction#cite_note-1. I would go further. Chapter 19 of this book deliberately incorporates elements of comic fantasy in general and hockey fantasy in particular. See *Goon* (2011). https://en.wikipedia.org/wiki/Goon_(film) or see *Slap Shot* (1977). https://en.wikipedia.org/wiki/Slap_Shot

She beams, clearly as proud of the young man I'm growing into as I am to be someone she can be proud of.

"I mean go on, child. You are inn-arresting!"

Not all players see ice-time in all situations. Some quarterback the power play. Others kill penalties. Still others dominate the face-off circle. Some are called who only drop the gloves.

Changing on the fly, I query my inner *Grove Dictionary of Music and Musicians*.

Ida Mae shovels me a soft pass in front of the crease.

Spouting trivia about how Noel set several of Countée's "Epitaphs" to music, along with poems by Gwendolyn Brooks, Langston and others, I blast a one-timer past the goalie from below the hash marks.

Shoots, *he* scores!

Ida Mae nearly leaps from her seat.

"Ain't that da troof!"

Stick raised rafterward in celebration, I look for applause out in the stands, where Noel sits behind the players' bench, smiling but otherwise noncommittal.

Problem is, I am precocious in the way immature writers often are: I can put all the right words in the right order but have no lived experience to draw from. Like Countée, I begin publishing in my teens. My first piece, appearing in Hemingway's *Kansas City Star*,[6] is a bombastic letter to the editor about prison reform written before I'd even spent a week in jail.

"He can coin some grand phrases," Zora tells Locke behind the back of a young writer who might as well be me, "but has that awkwardness of youth."[7]

Come to think of it, this scene takes place between the time Owen publishes *Come Home Early, Child* (1977) and *The Harlem Book of the Dead* (1978), his collaboration with Ida Mae's friend Camille Billops—"archivist, filmmaker, printmaker, sculptor, don't you know"—and photographer James Van Der Zee. Owen is down the hall conducting a telephone interview with National Public Radio before he makes his entrance.

6. Kevin Brown's first appearance in print.

7. Letter from Zora Neale Hurston to Alain Locke, quoted in *Zora Neale Hurston: A Life in Letters*.

"And Owen, of course, you know all about. Kevin here," Ida Mae pauses, dramatically, for the benefit of all in attendance, "knows *everything*."

Punishing check at center ice. Oohs and aahs from the crowd. Old Ida Mae hits me hard. She's just getting warmed up.

The arena's abuzz. Referee Edith Dodson waives off the call. Good, clean hit. No penalty. Let 'em play! Strong on my skates, I absorb the impact, and circle back, stick-handling, to buy some time, get a better read on the developing situation, figure out my next move, and keep the conversational puck in play.

"Mr. Dodson."

"Call me Owen, dammit."

I make the high-percentage play, skate back over to the bench, and quit while I'm ahead. For the remainder of the luncheon, I keep my smart mouth shut.

Second Period

Owen loved to cook, and hosted meals for both Countée and Du Bois. Whatever we had before the cheese course must have been very tasty, because Ida Mae spit her mouthpiece back into her glove, and said something like:

"Oooh wee! We eatin' *high* on the hog, child!"

After lunch, Owen invited me to his study. Ida Mae gave her blessing.

I must have been eighteen—five years older than Hilton Als was when he first encountered Owen. They'd ceased to be lovers by the time I finished high school, so my memory of Owen differs sharply from that depicted in *The Women*.

I don't remember Owen as the has-been Als describes: too young to be included in the Harlem Renaissance; insufficiently militant to be grouped with 1960s and 1970s playwrights like Ed Bullins or Amiri Baraka, Owen's former student at Howard University. I certainly don't remember him being intellectually lazy, because he was sharply critical of what he deemed a lack of intellectual curiosity on my part.

Physical disability doesn't linger in my mind as his distinguishing characteristic, even though hip-replacement operations required him to use a walker. My uncle wore a lift shoe just like Owen's, and walked with a pronounced limp. So, I scarcely noticed Owen was a "cripple."[8]

Ida Mae seemed unashamed Owen had struggled with alcoholism. I didn't know him well enough to tell the difference. For all I knew, he could have been performing with a hangover. My own dependence on alcohol grew gradually. Living in the Bay Area during my early twenties, I was a purely social, occasional-weekend-in-the-wine-country type drinker. After willing myself off drugs during my late twenties, throughout my thirties I dabbled in single-malts, which I sipped slowly while writing. In New York, my chaser of choice became a 12-ounce bottle of the Dominican pilsner, *Presidente*. Drinking in bars got to be both expensive and time-consuming, so I started drinking home alone. A prisoner of habits, I write every day, which meant drinking became routine, and an already high tolerance inherited from my father's side of the family heightened. Ergo, I drank too much. If I had a hangover in the morning, I simply spiked my iced cappuccino with a little Irish on the way in to work. By the time that high-functioning buzz wore off, it'd be time for lunch. For optimal effect, I'd slam an airliner-sized nip or shooter on an empty stomach before I wrote during lunch hour, which buzz might last till happy hour. By dinner time, I'd poured out the last of a half-pint of empty calories from whatever was 80-proof and cheap, usually vodka or whiskey but rarely gin, and chased that rot-gut liquor with a pint of Heineken, eaten a little something, or not, watched the *PBS News Hour* and/or a feature film or documentary, taken a sleeping pill, and gone to bed. Except when behaving belligerently and/or otherwise making a spectacle of myself, as I'd grown up ashamed to watch my mother do, I got to the point where nobody, not even I, could tell whether or not I was buzzed—buzzed drinking, buzzed driving—because I was always buzzed. Who am I to judge Owen for being an alcoholic just because, at a dinner party, he once barfed in his soup?

What I remember about meeting Owen Dodson was his frustration with my lack of initiative. He joined the Howard University faculty after finishing his MFA at Yale. Of others' or his own estimate of Owen's place in African-American theater history I have no idea. Because it never occurred to me to ask him. Like Ida Mae, Owen

---

8. Hilton Al's usage, from *The Women*. New York: Farrar, Straus and Giroux 1998.

was a raconteur, and probably would have told me anything I cared to know about his work with the Howard University Players and Alain Locke. He might even have told me, as Ida Mae certainly never would, the story of how Locke used to invite young men to his DC home, widely rumored to be haunted, in the Shaw West neighborhood, near Howard. He'd have them do a striptease to the accompaniment of classical music; then Locke would have them sit on the bed while he sprinkled coins all over their naked bodies.

"Lawd," Zora said, "Lawd, Lawd!"[9]

I was even more ignorant of art history than I was of theater history. I demonstrated no curiosity about what it must have been like to work alongside Lois Mailou Jones, who taught design and watercolor at Howard for forty-seven years, right up until my visit with Owen. I was reading George Bernard Shaw, who literally wrote the book on the essence of Ibsenism, but never once asked Owen for an account of turn-of-the-century New Drama or his production of *Ghosts*. Owen met Benjamin Britten in Brooklyn Heights after the War, but I didn't seem interested in what song cycles or opera projects the composer was writing with Peter Pears' voice specifically in mind. No wonder Owen was annoyed.

"You do know," Owen sighed, "that Arna taught at Yale?"

"I did *not* know that."

"You've visited Yale?"

"No."

"Why the hell *not*? It's less than two hours away!"

Another rookie mistake: I was so preoccupied with scoring goals that I hadn't developed into a two-way player, responsible in my own zone, playing a 200-foot game at both ends of the ice. I hadn't gone out of my way to read anything Owen had written. Yet asked him to read that novel I was writing. A copy of which is housed among Owen's papers at—where else?—Yale.

In 1977, a famously underrated actress portrayed Lady Macbeth in Orson Welles' production at the Henry Street New Federal Theater. I knew her only from roles in sitcoms like *Maude*.

"Tell me what you know about Esther Rolle."

"From *Good Times*?"

---

9. Letter from Zora Neale Hurston to Alain Locke dated March 20, 1933, quoted in *Zora Neale Hurston: A Life in Letters*, p. 282.

Exasperated, Owen smacked himself upside his highly Shavian forehead.

"From. Mac. *Beth*."

Had I even read Shakespeare? Which Off-Broadway or Off-Off Broadway productions did I intend to see?

I had no satisfactory answers to Owen's very pointed questions.

"What did you come to New York *for*," Owen's voice was stern with that youth-is-wasted-on-the-young reproach, "if not to take advantage of what it has to offer?"

I was out of my league.

My audition with drama coach Dodson was over.

Third Period

Owen delivered his scouting report to the theatrical troupe.

"He ain't ready yet."[10]

Brief silence. Then hoots of belly-laughter from the seats.

Edith waived off the call. No hit-from-behind or boarding. Let 'em play!

"Kevin here," Ida Mae paused just long enough for me to take my cue, excuse myself, and leave, "was just on his way to Penn Station. Weren't you, Kevin?"

"Penn *Station*? Where *you* goin'?"

"Washington."

"Washington! What on earth *for*?"

Captain Ida Cullen-Cooper diagrammed the play.

"He's going down to Howard; visit that Moorland-Spingarn Research Center, where Alain Locke's papers are held—isn't that what you said?"

I gritted my teeth; nodded my head.

"Yes, ma'am."

Ida Mae slurps her mouthpiece back in from her glove. Makes a mental checklist of literary chores for me to do.

"And, since you're going down to DC on a weekday," her voice takes on an urgency typically reserved for when she sends me on coupon-errands at the supermarket, "child, I want you to look up

---

10. Hatch, James V. *Sorrow Is the Only Faithful One: The Life of Owen Dodson*. Urbana and Chicago. University of Illinois Press (1991). See Chapter 15, "The Funeral."

Charles Cooney,[11] in the Manuscripts Division, over at that Library of Congress."

Ida Mae sensed my uncertainty about navigating Manhattan Island.

"Child, avenues run north and south. Numbered streets run perpendicular from that East River over to the Hudson. You get lost, just look up at the Empire State Building. That way, you always know where you are."

Ida Mae spits her mouthpiece back out into her glove.

"Go on! And *don't*," she winked around the table, really hamming it up for her fans, *"come home early, child!"*

They guff-*awed*, smacked their hands down on table, clutched at their sides, and dabbed their eyes with napkins.

*

Round about that time—when Lydia Davis was translating her first books and publishing her first volumes of short stories—I discovered how Proust, in *Swann's Way*, introduces all the characters who will occur, develop and recur throughout that great first-novel and *Within a Budding Grove*, how he introduces themes that rhyme with what's gone before and what's yet to come. Proust's ambition as novelist was "a desire to write a book that would rival Balzac's panorama of society[12] and to frame within that [frame] the intimate history of a young man's artistic and spiritual evolution."

The notion grew upon and gradually consumed me: preserving Ida Mae's past and that of her circle through World War I, the Great Migration, the Harlem Renaissance, the Great Depression, World War II, Vietnam, the Civil Rights Movement and on the 1960s counter-culture would be tantamount to chronicling my own future.

I abandon my own novel, forty-five years and two marriages ago, to begin my personal search for a usable past: the fiction you are now reading.

---

11. A real person, actually living at that time. Again, some things in this book might be misremembered half a century after the fact, but none of it is "made up." See, e.g., https://findingaids.loc.gov/exist_collections/ead3pdf/mss/2012/ms012182.pdf

12. White, Edmund. *Marcel Proust*. New York: Viking, 1999.

Ida Mae's oral imaginarium was not different things. It was one thing, indivisible and whole; what Eudora Welty calls a "sensory education."[1]

Tuckahoe and Park Avenue became virtual galleries of African and African-American art and culture: here a book by Langston, illustrated by Jake Lawrence; there a first edition of McKay's *Home to Harlem*, with cover art by Aaron Douglas. She owned varied artifacts: Benin bronzed heads; Dan masks; a painting by Beaufort Delaney; terra-cottas; a Hale Woodruff watercolor of medieval Chartres.

Ida Mae rewarded my curiosity with docent recollections.

"Hale Woodruff taught at NYU for *decades*, child. I take you down to the Village one day. Let you see his old apartment. Introduce you to his family."[2]

"And these," Ida Mae pointed out a pair of bookends, "Countée commissioned Augusta Savage to create." In Paris, poet and sculptor socialized during his Guggenheim Fellowship, from 1928 to 1930. During the Depression, in what Mary Schmidt-Campbell calls the continuing open university atmosphere of Harlem, Savage administered an eight-thousand-square-foot art school, the Harlem Community Art Center, where emerging artists like Jake and Romie were able to mix with established organizers like Doug, a decade or two their senior.[3] Savage had executed portrait busts of Weldon Johnson and Du Bois, Ida Mae explained, but many of her works were damaged, lost or simply destroyed because she couldn't afford to have the clay or plaster cast in bronze.

"Palmer Hayden's work," she continued, "was more traditional. He didn't go in for the abstract as much as some of the others did."

I freeze—like an infielder before the short-hop—in front an object: bright red, blue and black. "Circe Turns a Companion of Odysseus into a Swine." One of six closely supervised screen-prints

---

1. Welty, Eudora. *One Writer's Beginnings*. Cambridge, MA: Harvard University Press (1984), p. 10.

2. She did.

3. Schmidt-Campbell, Mary. *An American Odyssey: The Life and Work of Romare Bearden*. New York: Oxford University Press (2018).

from Bearden's 1977 *Odysseus Series*, signed, numbered and custom-framed, it was given to Ida Mae as a present by her loyal friend, and was on proud display in her Kip's Bay apartment.

As clearly as I see the imagery of Toomer's sound-collage *Cane*, I hear the collar-beads and bangles the Africanized sorceress' slender, near-naked figure adorns. Can see what John Edgar Wideman means when he writes, "All I really need to say is 'dance'."[4] Arms flail, feathered headdress preens, torso thrashes to the downbeat of something like "Adoration of the Earth" or "Sacrifice" from *The Rite of Spring*; right arm rises, up above the altar where a skull's displayed; phobic serpents coil, up the left; Circe summons forth spirits investing her with the power to step un-imprisoned through the frame.

"That," proclaims Ida Mae's proud, ancestral voice, startling me out of my trance, "is Romie."

"One day," the oracle continues, "you'll meet his wife, Nanette." Then, matter-of-factly, "lives down there on Canal Street, near Chinatown."[5]

*

Same year Jimmy began studying with Countée, Bearden graduated from New York University. Harlem Renaissance creative energies continually shifted from the hub to so-called satellites like Washington, DC. The end of one era marked the beginning of what Schmidt-Campbell, in *An American Odyssey: The Life and Work of Romare Bearden*, calls the "generational divide"[6] in black visual arts. Relatively new, the Museum of Modern Art mounted an exhibition of West African sculpture that year. Romie, says Schmidt-Campbell "was foreshadowing a generation of artists that succeeded those of the Harlem Renaissance."[7] Harlem is imaginable without Romare

---

4. Wideman, John Edgar. "Between the Shadow and the Act." Quoted in Robert G. O'Meally, ed. *The Romare Bearden Reader*. Durham: Duke University Press (2019), p. 210.

5. I finally got the chance to meet Nanette Bearden in her native Staten Island.

6. Schmidt-Campbell, Mary. *American Odyssey: The Life and Work of Romare Bearden*. New York: Oxford University Press (2018).

7. *Ibid.*, 83.

Bearden. But the Bearden of *The Block* (1971) is unimaginable without Harlem.

Haygood's *I, Too, Sing America* covers a wide variety of visual art, including films, and posters from the period, illustrating the varied ways performing artists as well as videographers continue fighting representational injustice. In keeping with the canon of African-American visual art, most names a generalist would expect to find in the index of such a book do in fact appear. Graphic artist Elizabeth Catlett, sculptor Meta Vaux Warrick Fuller, painters Malvin Gray Johnson, William Henry Johnson, and, as documentary portrait photographer, Carl Van Vechten.

Specialists might question the omission of Hale Woodruff, as mural painter, from a book that otherwise succeeds in illuminating both the development of the Harlem Renaissance as an artists' collective and the transnational evolution of individual artists. Bearden traveled to Atlanta to meet Woodruff. Bearden's earliest paintings, Schmidt-Campbell argues, were as influenced by Douglas and Woodruff as by the Mexican muralists. In *I, Too, Sing America*, Bearden is represented by *Untitled* (*Harvesting Tobacco*) (c. 1940), an early work done in what Schmidt-Campbell calls "a naturalistic, social realist style"[8] from the period that marks "the first flowering of Bearden's art."[9] A matron painted in gouache on brown paper recalls the women of Bearden's Southern childhood, "sturdy figures calm, the faces stoic and mask-like, bodies stiffly articulated and still, as if they were carved from wood. Painted in earth tones and with muted reds and blues,"[10] the colors are almost muddy: brownish-red ochres and greens.

Schmidt-Campbell argues that the "influence of Woodruff's murals has been overlooked in art history."[11] Woodruff's absence from the exhibition and accompanying volume, whatever the curatorial rationale, was as conspicuous as his accomplishments are undeniable. In 1936, muralist Diego Rivera granted Woodruff the historic

---

8. *Ibid.*, 54

9. Schwartzman, Myron. *Romare Bearden: Celebrating the Victory*. New York: Franklin Watts (1999), p. 53.

10. Schmidt-Campbell, Mary. *An American Odyssey: The Life and Work of Romare Bearden*. New York: Oxford University Press (2018).

11. *Ibid.*, 117.

opportunity to assist him and study in Mexico. The remaining two-thirds of Los Tres Grandes, José Orozco and David Alfaro Siqueiros, likewise influenced the thousands of hospital, library, post office, and school walls Woodruff and his African-American peers decorated. Later, Woodruff either established or was long-tenured in the art departments of historically black colleges like Atlanta University and predominantly white institutions like New York University, whose permanent collections he helped develop, thus creating what Schmidt-Campbell calls "an environment in which young painters, sculptors, and printmakers could thrive."[12]

Reception of Woodruff's day-glo *Amistad Murals* (1938–1942) has been mixed.[13] One could even argue, as critic Robert Hughes said of Rivera himself, that Woodruff was "a gifted painter deformed by the needs of propaganda. Sometimes his work was too openly didactic and coarse-grained, too attached to populist stereotypes."[14] Nevertheless, Schmidt-Campbell asserts that Hale Woodruff's legacy "was as consequential as that of any artist who lived and worked in New York."[15] Despite changing tastes, a definitive retrospective of early-twentieth-century African-American artists without Woodruff seems as unrepresentative as would a survey of Harlem Renaissance writers without Countée.

What is it in Romie's work that remains, decades after his death, the source of what Wallace Stevens calls "imperishable bliss"?[16]

A fitting complement to *An American Odyssey*, Robert G. O'Meally's *Romare Bearden Reader* gathers nearly three dozen previously uncollected pieces, eight of them artist's statements, book chapters, essays, journal entries, art reviews and speeches by Bearden himself dating from the mid-1930s to 1993.

---

12. *Ibid.*, 114.

13. For more about the by now centuries old conflict in African-American culture between aestheticism and political activism, see Huggins 202. Then again, "I do not care a damn," Du Bois thundered, "for any art that is *not* used for propaganda." Lewis 176.

14. Hughes, Robert. *Nothing if Not Critical: Selected Essays on Art and Artists* (Including "SoHoiad"). New York: Penguin (1992).

15. Schmidt-Campbell, Mary. *An American Odyssey: The Life and Work of Romare Bearden*. New York: Oxford University Press (2018).

16. Stevens, Wallace. "Sunday Morning," from *Harmonium*. New York: Knopf (1923).

The best guide on how to "read" a Bearden is Bearden. Gallery-goers and museum-goers, even those intimately familiar with his visuals, may not realize just how "literary" an artist Romie really was. His writer friends—James Baldwin, Ralph Ellison, Albert Murray, painter Derek Walcott—admired the way he might as casually refer to a sonnet by Drayton as he would to a painting by Titian. Bearden browsed bookstores with Murray, amassing an impressive library of his own. Too much the perfectionist to pursue writing as a mere hobby, Bearden devoted Tuesdays and Thursdays to reading and research, spending as much time in libraries and archives as he did in museums and galleries.

To put his writings in context, it helps to know when, where and why he published them. Romare Bearden's mother, Bessye Bearden reported for, and was a columnist and editor of *The Chicago Defender*, part of the national network of black daily newspapers like the *Baltimore Afro-American* (to which Romie later contributed political cartoons) and the *Pittsburgh Courier*.

During the Depression, when Bessye Bearden entertained dignitaries in her parlor less often than she might have wished, Roosevelt's WPA enabled young visual artists like Romie to collaborate with literary artists in the way he would the rest of his life. By age 23, Bearden had already assumed his rightful place in what Elizabeth Alexander calls a "literary continuum," contributing—both "in print," to quote Du Bois, "and in paint"—to "the African-American critical enterprise."[17]

Bearden's first essay appeared in Charles S. Johnson's Urban League publication *Opportunity*, for which Doug had designed cover art in the mid-1920s. From the "The Negro Artist and Modern Art"[18] to the posthumously published children's book *Li'l Dan the Drummer Boy*, Bearden's writings are in one way or another preoccupied with centuries-old, purely aesthetic questions of how two-dimensional media limited to horizontals and verticals can suggest a

17. Alexander, Elizabeth. "The Genius of Romare Bearden." Robert G. O'Meally, ed. *The Romare Bearden Reader*. Durham: Duke University Press (2019), p. 192.

18. Bearden, Romare. "The Negro Artist and Modern Art." *Opportunity: Journal of Negro Life*. XII (December 1934): 12. Robert G. O'Meally, ed. *The Romare Bearden Reader*. Durham: Duke University Press (2019), pp. 86-90.

third dimension without recourse to the illusion of mechanical per-spective or "mere photographic realism."[19] But in "The Negro Artist and Modern Art" we also encounter the political Bearden—an aspect of his art sometimes overshadowed by his connoisseurship, just as Bearden's reputation as colorist sometimes obscures what Mary Lee Corlett calls his "consummate skills as a draftsman, accentuating both the delicacy and the powerful simplicity of his lines."[20]

Bearden wrote prolifically from the age of twenty-three until his posthumous *A History of African-American Artists: 1792 to the Present* (1993). As he wrote, he "rethought completely his views about the nature of art and his role as an artist."[21] Albert Murray suggested to Bearden many of the evocative titles his works bear. In return, Bearden designed the book cover for Murray's novel *Train Whistle Guitar* (1977) as well as Dizzy Gillespie's autobiography *To Be or Not To Bop* (1978). The Limited Editions Club published Derek Walcott's *Poems of the Caribbean*, illustrated by Bearden watercolors and a lithograph. Similarly, Aaron Douglas had designed the dust jackets for Arna's *God Sends Sunday*, as well as several books by Countée, Claude McKay, and others, while Lawrence illustrated one of Langston's books.

Romie and Nanette visited the Caribbean for the first time in 1960. His friend Ida Mae wintered in St. Croix. With advancing age, each suffered during New York cold snaps, Ida Mae from Reynaud's disease.[22] Her nipples, nose, lips, earlobes, fingertips—despite the elegant gloves she always wore—throbbed and tingled painfully in the bitter cold. Romie suffered from a stiff back and aching joints. When he retired from his day job at the Welfare Department,[23] Romie began spending each February through March with Nanette on the Dutch/French island of St. Martin, where his watercolors lay drying in the sun.

---

19. *Ibid.*

20. Corlett, Mary Lee. "Impressions and Improvisations: A Look at the Prints of Romare Bearden," excerpt from *The Process to Print: Graphic Works by Romare Bearden* (2009); quoted in Robert G. O'Meally, ed. *The Romare Bearden Reader.* Durham: Duke University Press (2019), pp. 315-350.

21. Schmidt-Campbell, Mary. *An American Odyssey: The Life and Work of Romare Bearden.* New York: Oxford University Press (2018).

22. This condition runs in the family. My mother suffered from Reynaud's, and—even in Southern California—so do I.

23. Dorothy West also worked at the New York City Welfare Department.

By the time I entered high school, he'd begun making artwork from cut-outs of pre-painted construction-paper, cobalts and clarets, hues more saturated than his earlier pastels. The small but influential following he'd had been building among curators and collectors since the 1930s grew to the point where in the early 1970s Bearden finally received the recognition that had eluded him in past decades: a Guggenheim Fellowship; a solo retrospective at the Museum of Modern Art; election to the National Institute of Arts and Letters. Today, Bearden's work is performed everywhere—on the covers of recordings by Billie Holiday, Wynton Marsalis, Charlie Parker, and Max Roach.

Bearden was now a full-time painter with a winter home in the Caribbean, where he and his wife Nanette could escape New York winters. This change in circumstance benefited both his writing and his art. By the time I graduated high school, printmaking became one of the many ways in which Bearden was constantly reinventing his visual vocabulary.

A visual omnivore, Bearden was "first and foremost a student of painting."[24] He embraced but refused to limit himself exclusively to the African roots of his heritage. Schmidt-Campbell shows Bearden constantly testing himself in his work, "trying on then discarding one approach to painting after another,"[25] from Social Realism to Abstraction in the 1940s, from mid-1950s Cubism to the "the rip and tear"[26] of breakthrough collages like *Watching the Good Trains Go By* (1964). "Bearden was finding his way home by rediscovering black subject matter,"[27] she writes, "but home for him was as global as it was local; as black as it was white; North American, Middle Eastern, European, Asian, and African. Home was a battlefield and a fortress, a past and a future, and a way of seeing and knowing."[28]

24. Schmidt-Campbell, Mary. *An American Odyssey: The Life and Work of Romare Bearden*. New York: Oxford University Press (2018), p. 7.

25. *Ibid.*

26. Schmidt-Campbell, Mary. *An American Odyssey: The Life and Work of Romare Bearden*. New York: Oxford University Press (2018).

27. *Ibid.*, 12.

28. *Ibid.*

The "stylized black silhouettes"[29] of Bearden's late improvisations in French Caribbean blue, the *Odysseus Series* (1977) are set against dramatic effects of intensely saturated, cannily alternated lights and darks—"Home to Ithaca," for example. Based on Homer, they affirm black experience but transcend identity politics, "[a]s if Homer had been a Mediterranean-African bard"[30] and the settings were North African rather than Greek. "Strict and classical,"[31] these works combine what Bearden termed "spatial elegance"[32] with masses of "sonorous color"[33] in the manner of Matisse's *Jazz*.

The twenty "distinct yet unified works"[34] Richard Powell describes as comprising the *Odysseus* collages, some large-scale and others intimate, bear titles like "Cattle of the Sun," "Odysseus Leaves," "Poseidon," "The Sea Nymph," "Siren's Song," and "Troy Burning." Stark yet vibrantly saturated with color, sinuously geometric, they sing a Trojan War hero's roots, his departure, his wanderings, his shipwreck, his temptations and, finally, his homecoming. Possessed of both timelessness and dignity, conveying both action and repose, the *Odysseus Series* illustrates the conquest of the Mediterranean by successive waves of African, European and Semitic peoples, the great migrations, the trade routes and civilizations.

Bearden, fascinated all his life with manual laborers of the North Carolina cotton fields and Pittsburgh steel mills, showed up every day at his studio in blue overalls before 10 a.m. He painted a solid five or six hours for the last twenty years of his life, till just four days before his death.

More than a quarter-century after Bearden's death from bone cancer in 1988, when Ellison delivered his eulogy to the hundreds

29. Powell, Richard. "Changing, Conjuring Reality." Robert G. O'Meally, ed. *The Romare Bearden Reader*. Durham: Duke University Press (2019), p. 296.

30. Schwartzman, Myron. *Romare Bearden: Celebrating the Victory*. New York: Franklin Watts (1999).

31. Schmidt-Campbell, Mary. *An American Odyssey: The Life and Work of Romare Bearden*. New York: Oxford University Press (2018).

32. Bearden, Romare. *The Painter's Mind: A Study of the Relations of Structure and Space in Painting*. New York: Crown Publishing Group. (1969; 1981), p. 87.

33. *Ibid.*, 62.

34. Powell, Richard. "Changing, Conjuring Reality." Quoted in Robert G. O'Meally, ed. *The Romare Bearden Reader*. Durham: Duke University Press (2019), p. 210.

gathered at the Cathedral of St. John the Divine, Bearden's art authoritatively continues to transmute what Albert Murray calls "the idiomatic particulars of Afro-American experience"[35] into "aesthetic statements of universal relevance and appeal."[36] It's no surprise Bearden's "hugely resonant"[37] themes should be reflected both in the writers who influenced him and in those who never stop writing about him.

*

What could the *Odysseus* collages in general and "Circe" in particular, what could the art of a storyteller like Bearden have to teach a misguided novelist? What was the secret of narrative propulsion, of maximizing what Nabokov disparages as human interest, of reproducing *life* upon the page? How had Bearden done it?

John Edgar Wideman writes that Bearden's collages remind you of the way women who helped raise you talked. "Her stories flatten and fatten perspective. She crams everything, everyone, everywhere into the present, into words intimate and immediate as the images of a Bearden painting. When she's going good [she] manages to crowd lots and lots of stuff into a space that doesn't feel claustrophobic. She fills space to the brim without exhausting it."[38]

Even forty-five years ago, I knew it when I first saw Circe; knew, as August Wilson knew when he said that, in Bearden, he'd found an artistic mentor, and aspired to write plays the equal of Bearden's images, as Bearden himself knew, when he aspired to make images emulating what he heard between the notes of Earl ("Fatha") Hines' piano. I very much *wanted* to write something, but had no more idea

35. Schwartzman, Myron. "Sheer Mastery: Romare Bearden's Final Year." Robert G. O'Meally, ed. *The Romare Bearden Reader*. Durham: Duke University Press (2019), p. 361.

36. *Ibid.*

37. O'Meally, Robert G. "'Pressing on Life Until It Gave Back Something in Kinship,' An Introductory Essay," *The Romare Bearden Reader*. Durham: Duke University Press (2019), pp. 1- 28.

38. Wideman, John Edgar. "Between the Shadow and the Act." Quoted in Robert G. O'Meally, ed. *The Romare Bearden Reader*. Durham: Duke University Press (2019), pp. 209-216.

what to write than Romie, in the very early 1940s, knew whom to paint. I only knew I wanted to make writings that contained precise amplitudes, simple sonorities, and vivid clarity the way Bearden's *Odysseus* collages do. The raw material lay all about me. I had only to connect the dots.

Schmidt-Campbell notes that Bearden created a breathtaking range of female-power figures: "matriarchs; conjure women; religious icons of mother and child; the Virgin Mary with annunciate angel; women engaging in the everyday routine rituals of their lives; sensuous nudes, lounging and bathing; young women with older women; women with men or alone."[39]

I thought I'd already found my themes when Bearden became the subject of the first short book I contracted to write fourteen years after encountering "Circe." My true subject turned out to be this group portrait with Ida Mae's oral history narratives at its center and myself, as participant-observer, hovering about the periphery.

The spell Circe cast proved the right catalyst at the right juncture of time, place and readiness. I didn't inherit that artwork. I wasn't ready yet. What little money I eventually inherited was the merest honorarium. This generous bequest of material was Ida Mae's lasting endowment.

I'm almost ready now.

---

39. Schmidt-Campbell, Mary. *An American Odyssey: The Life and Work of Romare Bearden*. New York: Oxford University Press (2018), pp. 26-27.

21 A Valediction

Every so often, a poet like Arna, Sterling A. Brown, Countée or James Weldon Johnson would publish, almost before the ink had dried on what their contemporaries had written, anthologies redefining the canon of black poets from the United States.

A century ago, James Weldon Johnson's *Book of American Negro Poetry* (1922), followed by Countée's *Caroling Dusk*[1] and Sterling A. Brown's anthology, co-edited with Arthur P. Davis, *The Negro Caravan,* all agreed on thing: the key late nineteenth-century African-American figure is a poet whose parents were both slaves: Paul Laurence Dunbar.[2]

Today, Young's anthology, *African American Poetry: 250 Years of Struggle and Song,* is not only a new version, not just a revision. It's an alternative vision: what Lucille Clifton calls "a shift of knowing."[3]

One poet common to all of these anthologies is Countée Cullen.

For over one hundred years, Countée's admirers have been many. The 3,000 people attending his funeral, like the 3,000 who'd attended his wedding, demonstrate how widely recognized he was, not just in Harlem but in the global literary community.

Before he died, Countée said, "I want to be sure of having some sane and logical criticism (and that does not necessarily mean criticism favorable to me) to offset the purely emotional criticism that may have a tendency to prevail in some quarters."[4]

*

"Cown Tay," Ida Mae too often said, "was one the greatest poets ever lived, child." I've never believed this, but might have been more tactful about saying so. For me, Countée remains one of many American

---

1. In his Foreword Countée calls it "an anthology of verse by Negro poets rather than an anthology of Negro verse." Countée Cullen, *Caroling Dusk,* p. xi.

2. Early 46.

3. Clifton, Lucille. "Homage to My Hips," quoted in Kevin Young, ed. *African American Poetry: 250 Years of Struggle & Song.* New York: Library of America (2020), p. 419.

4. Molesworth 281.

poets book-ended between Anne Bradstreet and John Berryman's *Homage to Mistress Bradstreet*.

During one of our fights she shouted, pained and bewildered, "I swear 'fore God, child, I just don't *understand* you!"

Our temperaments clashed, but I now understand she was passing griot tradition down from one generation to another.

One source of tension between us was that she encouraged me to call Countée my great-grandfather. This genealogical little white lie I now see as extended-family Truth. "These," as Zora said, "are my people."[5] I grew up in blended, inter-generational, non-nuclear families, supported like young Robert Johnson by a far-flung network on both sides. I know what Annie ("Annye," pronounced Ah-nyay) C. Anderson means when she says, in *Brother Robert: Growing Up with Robert Johnson*, that she and Robert Johnson, while not blood-relatives, were very much kin. My *people*. *My* people. Mmm hmm![6]

I clung headstrong to stubborn fact. My mother's grandmother was Countée Cullen's widow by second marriage—nothing more, nothing less. But it's more complicated than that.

Artists encountered in our formative years have as profound an influence on our unique signature as later, more consciously assimilated influences do. An unsparing critic, Wallie Thurman admitted Countée's "extraordinary ear for music."[7] His love of classical forms, transmitted via books of children's verse like *The Lost Zoo*, published the year my mother was born and read to me over and over by her and by other women who helped raise me, have heightened my "physical awareness of the word"[8] in ways I'm probably not even aware of.

Countée is more than just somebody my great-grandmother married on the rebound. We aren't related by blood. But we are, in ways I hadn't even imagined, connected.

5. Hurston, Zora Neale, quoted in Fannie Hurst, "Zora Neale Hurston: A Personality Sketch." *Yale University Library Gazette* 35 (1961): 18.

6. Stone, Angie. "My People," featuring James Ingram, Idris Elba and Birdell Fitch contains elements from "My People" by Duke Ellington. https://en.wikipedia.org/wiki/The_Art_of_Love_%26_War.

7. Thurman, Wallace. "Negro Poets and Their Poetry." *Bookman*, July 1928, quoted in Jervis Anderson, *This Was Harlem: 1900-1950*, p. 206.

8. Welty, Eudora. *One Writer's Beginnings*. Cambridge, MA : Harvard University Press, 1984, p. 10.

My own opinion of Countée has come full-circle from early infat-
uation to premature disillusionment to abiding respect. I don't real-
ly see myself as a critic. I write from the standpoint of a practitioner,
understanding how masterpieces work, why they succeed or fail as
art—how their individual components interact, which works by one
artist relate to those of other artists—as opposed to what they might
or might not mean. I don't call this criticism. I call it reverse-engi-
neering. That's how Virginia Woolf became Virginia Woolf.

Here, my purpose is to strike a critical balance between extremes
of zealous and dismissive partisanship. At one extreme, zealots ar-
gue there's "no point in measuring [Cullen] merely beside Dunbar,"
as Clement Wood wrote; "he must stand or fail beside Shakespeare
and Keats and Masefield, Whitman, Poe and Robinson."[9] This is the
logical result of applying the letter and not the spirit of the law to
Countée's insistence on being judged first and foremost as a poet,
not a "negro poet."[10] For the moment, let's take him at his word.
Countée wouldn't have had it any other way.

The verse Countée published between the ages of fifteen and for-
ty-two coincides with an era Young outlines in *250 Years*, bookended
by Amy Lowell and Robert Lowell's *Lord Weary's Castle* (1946), which
appeared the year Countée died. Eliot published *Prufrock and Oth-
er Observations* (1917) in that pivotal year for African-American liter-
ature, when Claude McKay became among the first to publish e.e.
cummings in *The Liberator*.

Rappers and hip-hop artists may be fairer game in terms of com-
parison and contrast. So, let's leave Shakespeare and the Elizabe-
thans out of this. Poetry in English underwent yet another great
explosion, qualitatively and quantitatively, between World War I and
the death of Yeats. The US roster, to limit this discussion to po-
ets represented in *The Oxford Book of American Verse* (1950), is daunt-
ing: Conrad Aiken; Hart Crane; Randall Jarrell; Robinson Jeffers;
Marianne Moore; John Crowe Ransom; Delmore Schwartz; Wal-
lace Stevens; Allen Tate.[11] Then came the composer-lyricists—Fats

---

9. Wood, Clement. "The Negro Sings." *Yale Review* 15 (July 1926):824.

10. *The Brooklyn Eagle*, February 10, 1924. Quoted in Margaret Perry 16, citing
Jay Saunders Redding, *To Make a Poet Black* (Chapel Hill: University of North
Carolina Press (1929), p. 109.

11. "It was precisely because men like Wallace Stevens . . . T.S. Eliot, Conrad

Waller-Andy Razaf and too many others to name here—of the Great American Songbook.[12]

Countée's detractors are funnier than his admirers. Darryl Pinckney, in *The New York Review of Books*, said Countée was essentially a neo-romantic with a taste for classical forms, a traditionalist whose couplets tend to go "in one eye and out the other."[13] Even staunch supporters note a tendency toward sentimentality in Countée's verse. His weakest poems, Molesworth says, "are clumsy and the symbolism . . . clichéd."[14] They are "facile," "rather stilted . . . laden with medieval and courtly imagery"[15] and "excessively archaic language." [16] At this critical extreme, Countée is seen as a mere reactionary of no great depth or originality, a sonneteer whose lyrics rise only sporadically above the level of undergraduate effusion—a second-rate Edna St. Vincent Millay, a lost Keats.[17] Wallie Thurman accused Countée of sacrificing originality to mere virtuosity, genuine depth of feeling to grandiloquence.[18]

Seen in this context during my disenchantment phase, Countée wasn't my idea of a first-rate artist by any "sane and logical"[19] standard. Reading him alongside poets I began discovering in *The Oxford*

Aiken, E.E. Cummings [sic], and Malcolm Cowley knew that they 'belonged' by birth and training that they could dare [to] adventure." Huggins 229.

12. "The Great American Songbook is the loosely defined canon of significant early-20th-century American jazz standards, popular songs, and show tunes." https://en.wikipedia.org/wiki/Great_American_Songbook

13. Pinckney, Darryl. "The Sweet Singer of Tuckahoe." *New York Review of Books* (March 5 1992).

14. Molesworth 250.

15. Molesworth 88.

16. *Ibid.*

17. Wolfert, Helen. "Cullen's Early Poems Are Best." n.p. *Book Review Section* (16 March 1947):6-7.

18. Wallace Thurman says, "there is hardly anyone writing poetry in America today who can make the banal sound as beautiful . . . . [Cullen's] race poems, when he attempts to paint a moral, are inclined to be sentimental and stereotyped. It is when he gives vent to the pagan spirit and lets it inspire and dominate a poem's form and context that he does his most impressive work. His cleverly turned rebellious poems are also above the ordinary. But there are not enough of these . . . ." Early 47.

19. Molesworth 281.

Book of English Verse: 1250–1918 and anthologies like Young's, I imagined I'd outgrown his work.

I see things differently now. The progress of traditions and individual talents isn't linear. It's always spiraling in a state of constant flux, both outward from and backward towards a center. Today, I see continuity, not hierarchy, in the careers of Countée and his contemporaries, predecessors and successors during the years Ida Mae knew them.

Young's anthology demonstrates that expressing nuanced feeling and thought within the strict confines of sonnets and quatrains and without undue distortion of syntax is harder than it looks. Countée shares with Tate a conviction that classical forms have life left in them; that the trick is to make their content "appear natural," as Molesworth says, "even easy."[20]

A careful student of Tennyson, Countée infused iambic pentameter with metrical devices (enjambment, runover lines) designed to heighten the illusion of natural speech. Countée's vocabulary is a vibrant admixture of plain Anglo-Saxon and more abstract words of Greek, Latin or French origin. His uses of classical myth and biblical allusion, of slang and subjunctive, of thee and thou, his shades of coloring, changes in pitch and angles of attack are skillful and varied.

To the eye swiftly scanning the page, Countée's formalism may seem monotonous. But read aloud with the proper emphases, a poem like "She of the Dancing Feet" is all eye-rolling, head-swiveling, lip-smacking, finger-wagging swagger and street-sass. The economy and bite of satiric epitaphs from *Color*, full of human foibles and human kindness, consciously recall Horace, Juvenal, Martial and what Molesworth calls "other Latin poets who used epigrammatic forms."[21]

Because he'd aspired to succeed as both novelist and playwright, Countée's storytelling flair in narrative short-verse forms squeezes from any given quatrain every iota of dramatic tension—tensions of action, characterization, description, dialogue, humor, pathos, plot, point of view, scene and transition—that you can possibly squeeze from just thirty-two beats. At their very best, Countée's verses speak with both the authority of the pulpit and the intimacy of the salon.

---

20. Molesworth 70.

21. *Ibid.*

Naturalness is among his highest achievements. The wonder isn't that he sometimes fell short of it, but that he attained it as often as he did. Some of Countée's sonnets, still fresh nearly a century after their appearance, also rank among his most enduring achievements. Over-represented in classroom textbooks, under-representative poems like "Incident" are part of the reason he remains alive and well but under-appreciated as an artist.

Whatever the unevenness of his work as a whole, Countée's impact on African-American culture is greater than the sum of his best poems. Countée was emblematic of a flashpoint in global black literature the likes of which could only have occurred in a select few places at that particular time—Harlem and Washington, DC among them. "Countée was never fully understood as a poet or a writer," Gerald Early argues, "because he has never been fully understood as a man."[22]

Is Countée's so-called failure as poet to live up to perhaps unrealistic expectations after what Jessie Fauset called such "a brave and beautiful beginning"[23] somehow synonymous with failure in life? No. It's not always the very greatest artists who have the deepest influence on our development. So, does it matter whether Countée is considered a major or minor poet? His time was short. His reach exceeded his grasp; but Robert Browning said that's what heaven's for. As for his work, if there's a place in the canon of American poetry for many the minor figures represented in F.O. Matthieson's *Oxford Book of American Verse*, then there's a place for Countée, first and foremost as a poet, not just a negro poet. As for his life, it was a qualified success by any humane measure.

*

"Even the most incorrigible maverick," Baldwin wrote, "has to be born somewhere. He may leave the group that produced him—he may be forced to—but nothing will efface his origins, the marks of which he carries with him everywhere. I think it is important to know this and even find it a matter for rejoicing."[24]

---

22. Early 6.

23. Perry 27, citing Jessie Fauset in *The Crisis* 31 (March 1926):238.

24. Baldwin, James. "The Discovery of What It Means to be an American." From *Notes of a Native Son. Collected Essays.* New York. Library of America (1998).

Naturally, my principled stance on Countée's relative place in literary history provoked anger and resentment in Ida Mae. Of *course* she took umbrage at my matter-of-fact attempts to disabuse her notion of his Greatness. At the time, I suspected her of over-identifying with him. Even her neat and flowery handwriting—with long dashes at the ends of a sentence—began to resemble his. I now think I misjudged Ida Mae's defensiveness. I now see her the way Tatyana Tolstaya saw Joseph Brodsky.

"He had an extraordinary tenderness for all his . . . friends, generously extolling their virtues, some of which they did not possess. When it came to human loyalty, you couldn't trust his assessments—everyone was a genius . . . . for him, a human bond was higher than justice, and love higher than truth."[25]

From Ida Mae's point of view, History was made at the crossroads of both individual and materialist forces, by artists in solidarity, not lone-wolves-in-exile like Toomer or McKay. Maybe she saw my resistance to her cultural agenda as some kind of Oppositional Defiant Disorder (ODD).

Should I have been more tolerant of her loyalist oversimplifications, less concerned with winning arguments than with clarifying positions? Sure. Ida Mae—though good, well-meaning—was not always patient, kind. Her fuse shortened as she aged. She was every bit as ambitious as Countée, as controlling as Alain Locke, as intelligent as Dorothy West, as shrewd as Charles S. Johnson, and had as acute a sense of historical mission as Arna. Nor was she above petty vindictiveness. Changed codicils like fur coats. Could the heated exchanges, the sullen silences, the battle of wills have been avoided? I'm not so sure. Maybe the rupture between Ida Mae and me wasn't a question of whether. Maybe it was just a question of when.

"Anyone," says Aristotle, "can become angry—that is easy; but to be angry with the right person, to the right degree, at the right time, for the right purpose, and in the right way—that is not easy."[26]

25. Tolstaya, Tatyana, translated from the Russian by Jamey Gambrell. "On Joseph Brodsky (1940–1996)." *New York Review of Books*. February 29, 1996. https://www.nybooks.com/articles/1996/02/29/on-joseph-brodsky-19401996.

26. Aristotle on Anger. https://www.forbes.com/quotes/642/

22 Sterling A. Brown: Broad Noon Daylight

I

Countée's fame can never again be what it was, nor what Langston's is now. But the question isn't whether Countée or Langston is the better poet. The question isn't even which aesthetic, Langston's free-form or Countée's classicism, relative to their respective lines of literary descent—Walt Whitman-William Carlos Williams versus W.B. Yeats-W.H. Auden—is inherently superior. The question in certain quarters is whether either poet of the so-called Harlem Renaissance rivals Sterling A. Brown, whose poems some think more resonant than Countée's, more varied than Langston's.

Dozens of Old Guardians and Young Turks have published memoirs and/or had multivolume biographies written about them. Which perhaps explains why they remain better known to general readers than does Sterling A. Brown.

"The Dark Tower," Part III of Young's anthology, covers the period 1919–1936, roughly corresponding to the Harlem Renaissance era. *The Collected Poems of Sterling A. Brown,*[1] superimposed upon *African American Poetry: 250 Years of Struggle and Song*, restores visibility to a central figure in African-American literary history.

Think of Sterling Brown as midpoint along a timeline. James Weldon Johnson and Dunbar precede him. Melvin Tolson, Langston, Countée and their many female contemporaries are coeval. Robert Hayden and scores of others succeed him.

That genius ear for southern speech, that all-seeing eye on southern history, that perfect pitch—to name just three things that make Sterling Brown inimitable—were passed from father to son. Sterling Brown is a poet whose body of work, exploring the relationship between humans and their environments natural and built, combines folklore with a vivid sense of character, sense of place, sense of history and sense of swing.[2]

---

1. Selections from *The Collected Poems of Sterling A. Brown*, selected by Michael S. Harper. Copyright© 1980 by Sterling A. Brown. Reprinted by permission of the John L. Dennis Revocable Trust.

2. Locke, Alain. "Negro Youth Speaks," *The New Negro*, p. 52.

II Folklore & Folkways

Sterling Allen Brown, Countée's contemporary, spent summers down on a farm, off Whiskey Bottom Road, in Howard County, Maryland. The Reverend Sterling Nelson Brown, the poet's father, was born a slave in eastern Tennessee. Sterling Nelson's mother had her firstborn sold into slavery. Yet Sterling Nelson wasn't anxious to distance himself from this slave heritage. On the contrary, he celebrated the folklore and folkways of blacks rooted in slavery, influences as crucial to Sterling Allen's poetic development as the classical texts and languages, Anglo-Saxon and Beowulf, Molière and Shakespeare, he studied at Williams College or Harvard University three years before Countée earned his master's there.

The Reverend Brown was a Professor of Divinity at Howard University. Sterling Allen was born on campus and, except for brief sabbaticals at places like Atlanta University, New York University, Vassar College or Yale University, Sterling Brown spent his entire career at Howard, living in the Brookland neighborhood, in Northeast Washington, DC His poems reflect his wide travels, not only among the turpentine jook joints of Lower Dixie but also within the confines of Brookland.

Zora conducted oral history interviews with voodoo witchdoctors, filed anthropological field reports and ran amok with calipers used for measuring negroid craniums. Much of Brown's field work, though fundamentally serious, consisted of loafing among liars and *philosophes* of barbers shops, pawn shops and pool halls, where to this day the only recognizable English is behind the eight ball. Larger-than-real-life characters—Mrs. Bibby, Calvin ("Big Boy") Davis, Slim Greer—became the personae of his most admired poems.

An admirer of Dunbar, Countée nevertheless viewed dialect poetry—the depiction of black speech via mere orthographic ticks, dropped consonants, phoneticized spellings, truncated gerunds—as at best limited and at worst in poor taste.[3] By the time he died, worn out, aged thirty-three, Dunbar was pigeon-holed by editors and publishers as a poetaster who put his talent into King Edward VII's English and his genius into dialect. But for poets like James

---

3. As far as Cullen was concerned, "the day of dialect as far as Negro poets are concerned is on the decline." "Countée Cullen Plans Anthology," New York: *Amsterdam News*, 17 November 1926.

D. Corrothers, Ishmael Reed and Thomas Sayers Ellis, Dunbar remains emblematic.

African-American poetry published in Dunbar's era, between the 1890s and World War I, reflects centuries-long creative tensions between an oral/improvisatory culture of congregationally licit gathering and dangerously clandestine through-composed writing by slaves barred from literacy, "who lived in dread of the singing whip."[4] Early twentieth-century American verse, black or otherwise, embracing or rejecting dialect, can be seen in terms of a general trend away from the nineteenth-century Romantic and Victorian vestiges Countée only seems to rear-guard, and toward the depiction of a life more ordinary, in a language closer to everyday speech.

This vernacular of African-American migrants to urban centers like Columbus, Ohio, c. 1910–1940, like the African American visual art that mirrors it, represents the dialectic, as Schmidt-Campbell calls it, between life in the industrialized North and the rural South. This vernacular was to various degrees embraced by Robert Frost, A. E. Houseman, Vachel Lindsay, Edgar Lee Masters, Edwin Arlington Robinson, Carl Sandburg and William Carlos Williams. For Weldon Johnson, black dialect isn't the problem; the problem is its misuse. There is no appropriation, only misappropriation. For Johnson, African-American poets comic or otherwise, were held like any other American poet to the highest standards of ambition, the subtlest shades of thought and the greatest depths of feeling demanded by the varieties of human experience.[5]

Politically subversive, Dunbar feints with humor in "An Antebellum Sermon."

---

4. "who lived in dread of the singing whip," hereinafter, all quotes are from *The Collected Poems of Sterling A. Brown* unless otherwise indicated. "Memo: For the Race Orators," p. 232, Part I, line 5.

5. "All Americans, white as well as black, were provincials of a European tradition, Anne Bradstreet no less than Phyllis Wheatley, Thomas Nelson Page no less than Charles Wadell Chestnutt. But Negroes, being one notch further removed from 'belonging,' were less likely (or less quickly) to gain the perspective that would show the way to transform their own experience into art, free from . . . past formalism and manner. Negro literature and art, of course, was to free itself, just as the general American art and letters had during the war years, but that would come in the 1930s and after." Huggins 232.

But fu' feah someone mistakes me,
I will pause right hyeah to say,
Dat I'm still a-preachin' ancient,
I ain't talkin' 'bout to-day. . . .
Now don't run an' tell yo' mastahs
Dat I's preachin' discontent.

For Sterling Brown, Dunbar remains among the first but would not be the last American writer to accomplish fullness of scope and depth of insight in depicting the black experience.

Toomer sojourned in Sparta, Georgia, returning to his roots to create that classic hybrid of lyric prose, poetry and dramatic narrative known as *Cane*, which influenced Sterling Brown. So much so that when *Cane* appeared Sterling Brown lived among the folk, first as a lecturer in English at Virginia Theological Seminary and College at Lynchburg, located in Southampton County, and later at the historically black Lincoln University in Jefferson City, before returning to this own roots at Fisk, in Nashville. By day, he taught. On weekends and during summers, he mingled with backwoods Virginians, met their kinfolk, shared their vittles and their sweat. In those parts of the Deep South, where their ancestors were born and slaved or sometimes owned slaves themselves, both Brown and Toomer—like Du Bois and James Weldon Johnson before them—had their eyes opened to the vibrantly tesserated mosaic of black folk culture you see in Bearden's "Quilting Time" (1986).[6]

After years of teaching further afield, Sterling Brown was appointed to a position at Howard University. During the Depression, the Federal Writers' Project hired him as its Negro Affairs Director. Brown had watched ethnomusicologist Alan Lomax make field recordings under auspices of the Library of Congress—ballads, protest songs, chain-gang work songs, spirituals, gospel hymns, nitty-gritty-dirt-blues, early jazz and its folk-music accompaniments, campfire songs sung by black regiments like the First South Carolina Volunteers.

An oral historian's oral historian, Sterling Brown had prodigious natural talent nurtured by years of disciplined study from live models. Lomax had designed an oral history questionnaire. Ster-

---

6. See Romare Bearden, "Maquette for Quilting Time," 1985. https://dia.org/collection/maquette-quilting-time-34127

ling Brown modified it in such a way that the dozens of Federal Writers' Project workers he editorially supervised could use it in dozens of states, conducting field work documenting the oral history of ex-slaves—their half-remembered African chants, their aphorisms, their campfire songs of black regiments "chanted underneath the stars."[7] This folk literature forms the basis of Brown's body of work.

And though Sterling Brown didn't object to the label folk poet, it's useful to think of him as hybrid. In Sterling Brown, dialect is a form of what Dana D. Nelson calls oral literacy—folk wisdom. Plainly, Sterling Brown is laughing with destiny's fools, not laughing at them. Sterling Brown portrays black life the way that life sees itself, not as it continues to be pathologized in the media. Read back to back, Brown's "Ma Rainey" sounds very much like a riff on Dunbar's "When Malindy Sings." One suspects Sterling Brown, in "An Old Woman Remembers," of channeling a poem memorializing the race-riot Du Bois' denounced in "The Litany of Atlanta." It seems reasonable to read Brown's "Sister Lou" as channeling James Weldon Johnson.

There's nothing folksy about Sterling Brown's folkways. He respects his material too much to be pulling stunts , as Woolf accuses Joyce of doing in *Ulysses*. He took as genuinely respectful an attitude toward the folkways he encountered in the South as we should take toward Sterling Brown.

III A Sense of Character

Apart from Dunbar, whom did Sterling Brown model his work after? Sterling Brown was a close student of Molière, aka the French Menander. Congreve, aka the English Molière, was a student of Ben Jonson's Comedy of Humors. Think of Character in the 17th century sense of a moraliste like La Bruyère or a Greek natural philosopher like Theophrastus, whom La Bruyère translated. Theophrastus is best known for thirty fictional sketches known collectively as *Characters*. Each illustrates a dominant attribute or flaw or vice. Theophrastus' thirty characters are extreme types, whether deficient or excessive.

Think of Theophrastus' influence on Greek stage comedy and it's easy to see how this tradition, filtered down to a poet like Ster-

---

7. "chanted underneath the stars," "Virginia Portrait," line 37, p. 44.

ling Brown, survives in sketch comedy. Two outrageous Martin Lawrence types include "Romie Rome" or "Sheneneh." Jamie Foxx plays Cornbread Turner, with his dead-dog sidekick Duke Jeremy Jolly Rancher Remington Steele Louis Cadbury the third to the fourth power. By his own admission, Sterling Brown's characters were intended as American types in general and African-American types in particular. Old Comedy, New Comedy, black comedy—it doesn't matter. These types are perennial.

Sterling Brown's psychological vignettes are no less penetrating for being broadly satirical, even cartoon-like. They seldom lapse into caricature or parody. Because the action microscopes the characteristic essence and the characteristic essence telescopes the action. Hence the extreme economy of Sterling Brown's sequences—character, dialogue, scenes, situations. It's due in part to such type-casting that Sterling Brown's characters attain the condition of universality, irrespective of their blackness.[8] Sterling Brown's characters, engaged in what might on the surface seem like what LaTasha N. Nevada Diggs calls "coon bidness,"[9] are relatable people.

Working from specific to general and vice versa, Brown broadstrokes his characters, even those modeled on real life, as Theophrastan types—bumbler and grumbler, braggart, chatterbox, flatterbox, country bumkin, moaner and groaner, fatalist, cynic, rumor-monger, young fool, old fool, curmudgeon, huckster, shuckster, spendthrift, penny-pincher, preachin' man, do-right man, music man, workin' man, drankin' man, gamblin' man.

Slim Greer is the central character from Sterling Brown's classic series-satire of five poems: (1) "Slim Greer"; (2) "Slim Hears 'The Call'," "Slim in Atlanta," "Slim in Hell," and "Slim Lands a Job?" Greer is a barber-shop habitué familiar to everybody who's seen Eddie Murphy and Arsenio Hall in *Coming to America*. The bow-

---

8. Sterling A. Brown's genius is measured by how far he exceeds Huggins critique of mass African-American culture in particular and American mass culture in general. "After all, [Negroes] were Americans and affected by the good and bad taste of their countrymen. Like other Americans, blacks knew a commercial success—even when they might not know whether or not it was good—and their entertainment was tailored to the standards of mass culture." Huggins 293.

9. Diggs, LaTasha N. Nevada, quoted in Young, p. 933.

ing-and-scraping, "yessuh"–"nawsuh" type Old Lem represents harborers of dreams deferred.

Through travels North and South, from New Negro Chicago to Ole Miss and back, Sterling Brown peopled his human comedy with an entire range of Theophrastans who rise above cardboard type—"browns and yellers,"[10] buck dancers, break dancers, Harlem streetwalkers on the stroll, cracker "rebs"[11] and "damnyanks,"[12] field niggers both urban rural, "hangtailed hounds,"[13] share-croppers of every color, separated only by an 18-ft. cut of railroad tie, who die wid they toes turnt t'ward Dixie, women-folk hongry "for more then the men they know,"[14] Hebrews and Anglo-Saxons, village half-wits, overeducated snowflakes[15] and na'chal mans. There is Big Boy Davis, railroad man, troubadouring guitar player and coal miner whose homage is chanted, in work song-rhythm, in the chain-gang ballad "Southern Road." Big Boy recurs in "Long Gone."

Brown combines the ear for dialogue, characterization and dramatic timing he saw at the Old Howard Theater, at 7th and T Streets in DC. His knack for description in general and stop-time description in particular is astonishing.

In "Roberta Lee," a sassy chorine politely invites a contemptuous daughter of the Confederacy to kiss her black ass:

> To the rose of Dixie, to Roberta, Southerner,
> The chorine presented, due South, a Southern exposure.[16]

In "The Last Ride of Wild Bill," all whoopin' and hollerin,' you almost hear "Yakety Sax," the novelty-tune soundtrack to *The Benny Hill Show* antics, complemented with Sterling Brown's telegraphed image of a "masticated stogie butt."[17] The poetry of Sterling Brown

---

10. Razaf, Andy. "Black and Blue," quoted in Young, p. 240, line 7.

11. cracker "rebs," quoted in "An Old Woman Remembers," line 16, p. 217.

12. "damnyanks," quoted in, "Roberta Lee," line 8, p. 193.

13. "hangtailed hounds" quoted in "Old Lem," line 44, p. 209.

14. . . . . women-folk hongry "for more then the men they know," quoted in "Side by Side," Part VI, line 9, p. 255.

15. "Snowflake" is street slang for an overeducated black person , as in the 1989 film *Glory*.

16. "Roberta Lee," lines 31–32, p. 193.

17. "The Last Ride of Wild Bill," Part IV, line 17, p. 149.

isn't all slapstick and sight-gag humor. "Riverbank Blues" is almost Dunbaresque in its pastoral tone, its characters talkin' quiet, quiet lak an' slow.

High and low characters mingle, comingle and intermingle in Sterling Brown, a virtuoso ventriloquist who switches easily back and forth between registers, speaking from behind a wide variety of masks. These uncanny likenesses owe as much to the eye as to the ear. In "The Temple," we hear Harlem street-corner orators, race-men ranting in West-Indian dialects Derek Walcott and Eric Walrond would instantly recognize.[18] But Brown was no more exclusively a dialect poet than was Dunbar.

In addition to ballads, Sterling Brown experiments with blues rhythms and refrains, with traditional poetic forms he would have encountered at Williams College—the sonnet, villanelle, the eighteenth-century French popular song by Madame de Pompadour, *Nous n'irons plus au bois*, also a sonnet. Sterling Brown is both folk poet and lyric poet. "To a Certain Lady, in Her Garden" is a traditionally English pastoral. "Call Boy," is an experiment in d-rhymed octet. There are experiments in free verse, as in "Virginia Portrait." A series of ten blues triplets and doubled-triplets, "Choices" follows the pattern aaa/bbb.

Sterling Brown's *Collected Poems* are peopled thick with suitors crooning each other sweet "lies of love everlasting."[19] Even if his father hadn't been one himself, there'd have been deacons and preachers in Sterling Brown's work. There are also scoundrels/hustlers, often appearing in the same preacher-man guise/disguise. There are firemen on Southern rails, working dirty jobs for good pay—pay so good poorer whites would literally kill for those jobs. There are Mississippi riverboat troubadours, in poems like "Call Boy." Sometimes any or all of these will appear in a single poem like "Memphis Blues." Sometimes, the character will be blue collar; sometimes the character wouldn't be caught dead working a job that might break an impeccably manicured nail.

---

18. An Anglo-Caribbean born in British Guiana (1898), raised in Panama and educated the English way in colonial schools, Eric Walrond arrived in New York in 1918, just as Cullen was entering DeWitt Clinton. He staked his claim to the Renaissance, saying that Harlem was a "sociological El Dorado." Lewis 164.

19. "Children's Children," line 8, p. 117.

Types occur and recur. Working back from the general to the specific, one such type, the Dandy, whom Oscar Wilde would easily recognize, represents the pinnacle of what Sterling Brown calls "sartorial excellence."[20] Sportin' Daniels appears in *Southern Road* as Sporting Beasley, with "his patent leathers with his silk handkerchief."[21] There's old Scrappy, in his silk shirt, suspenders and brogans.

In real life Sterling Brown's colleague at Howard University, Alain Locke, was an uber-dandy, "so cosmopolitan," said Countée, "of thought and speech."[22] Surely, Locke was well aware of if not at all self-conscious about the figure he cut in his native Philadelphia as he contemplated the Impressionist painters. In Berlin, which he loved "much better than Paris,"[23] you might hear him discourse upon the monuments of the Tiergarten. And surely he realized that, even in a place as profligate of pimps as Harlem, he invited stares as he tapped his walking stick hurriedly along Lenox Avenue, nattily dressed in his gray suit with matching kid gloves, gray spats strapped over custom-made, cap-toe shoes—even his irises were matching gray—on the way downtown to meet W.E.B. Du Bois for luncheon.

*

African American Poetry: 250 Years of Struggle and Song features a dozen or more contributors who are Harvard University graduates. But in Sterling Brown's and Locke's day, even with an advanced degree from the University of Berlin or Oxford, a black Harvard man couldn't teach at Harvard. An unintended consequence of such segregation in higher-education was the concentration, at places like Howard University, where Sterling Brown taught for fifty years, of a caliber of talent and intellect later diffused throughout the nation. Sterling Brown, in fact, attended Paul Laurence Dunbar High School, then one of the most rigorous and prestigious of all DC public schools, and was mentored there, as Toomer had been before him, by poets

---

20. Sound-booth quip of Sterling A. Brown reading from *The Poetry of Sterling Brown*, recorded on various dates between 1946–1973, released on *Smithsonian Folkways* (1995).

21. "Sporting Beasley," line 25, p. 122.

22. Countée Cullen, "Millennial", quoted in Major Jackson, ed. *Collected Poems of Countée Cullen*. New York: Library of America, (2013), p. 105.

23. Letter from Alain Locke to Carl Van Vechten dated 27 July, no year.

Anne Spencer and Jessie Fauset, who in an era less wasteful of human capital could easily have been a university professor.

Hard to tell which was more tightly wound, Locke or his English umbrella. Some describe his manner as a mixture of prissiness and violent haste. At Howard University, Locke drilled students fussily, in German, and in Greek. His conversation was brisk. His strolls were brisk. His solicitations were brisk, as were his fallings out. Self-assured to the point of arrogance, impatient to the point of tyranny, Locke had "opinions," biographers say, that were "seldom equivocal."[24] It must have given Jessie Fauset great pleasure to note that so towering a figure wasn't even five feet tall.

Zora called him a "spiteful little snot"[25] but, despite very real flaws, Locke is the one character, who converging and crisscrossing with the paths of others, most contradicts first impressions, and comes unexpectedly to life. A more tolerant view of Locke is that he was a frustrated artist. He'd published relatively little, that little falling short of his grandiose expectations. The field of black studies had yet to be officially recognized, even at an historically black university like Howard, and dean Locke was powerless to institute it. So there, for all his brilliance, Locke languished between bouts of depression, ever expectant of "the shock of beauty,"[26] a scholar without a recognized specialty, a philosopher without a major philosophy, an artist without a form, wasting precious time and talent on one disappointing amorous intrigue after another, his little heart weak from an early age due to rheumatic fever.

From his throne in Washington, the old girl (as Locke privately saw himself) would

Alain LeRoy Locke. Painting by Betsy Graves Reyneau, from 1941–1963. Public domain.

24. Quoted in Leonard Harris & Charles Molesworth, *Alain L. Locke: The Biography of a Philosopher.* Chicago: University of Chicago Press (2008).

25. Letter from Zora Neale Hurston to James Weldon Johnson dated 1937, Yale University archives. Hemenway, p. 242.

26. Fabre, Michel. *From Harlem to Paris: Black American writers in France, 1840–1980.* Urbana and Chicago. University of Illinois Press (1991), p. 126.

lord it over wayward disciples in the arts—blues/jazz musicology, drama, fiction, nonfiction and poetry, proclaiming Harlem capital of the black race. As far as Locke was concerned, the black experience, when he published *The New Negro*, had at last emerged "from the age of discussion to the age of expression."[27]

I can't say how expectations this high must have affected Myron O'Higgins or other Sterling Brown students. I can only show what it was like for me.

The gravitational pull of Howard University's orbit is hard to overstate. Sterling Brown's sense of inherited tradition was as keen as his sense of duty toward transmitting it forward. Younger writers, performing artists and political leaders like Amiri Baraka, A.B. Spellman, Toni Morrison, Kwame Ture (Stokely Carmichael), Kwame Nkrumah, Thomas Sowell, Ossie Davis and many others were beneficiaries of Sterling Brown's pioneering studies in black folklore. Sterling Brown would have been Sterling Brown without Dudley Randall. Would Dudley Randall have been Dudley Randall without Sterling Brown?

In Young, we get a sense of how *250 Years* contributors read— riff on—the canon of African-American literature Sterling Brown practically codified. Paul Laurence Dunbar's "Sympathy" anticipates Maya Angelou; Amiri Baraka's "Preface to a Twenty Volume Suicide Note" harks back to Frank Horne's "Notes Found Near a Suicide," an Edgar Lee Masters-like evocation of a voice from beyond the grave. The "To One Who Called Me Nigger" section of Horne's poem is not just contemporaneous with Countée's "Incident" but also looks back, as does Countée himself, to the *Spoon River Anthology*.

IV A Sense of Place

It's essential to know how rooted in real life Brown's characters are. It's equally important to know how rooted those characters are in real places. Whether or not Sterling Brown truly belongs to the Harlem Renaissance is a moot point. True, millionaire New York hosts A'Lelia Walker and Carl Van Vechten were crucial in helping black artists social-network with white counterparts in uptown and downtown

---

27. See, generally, Locke, Alain, ed. *The New Negro: Voices of the Harlem Renaissance*. New York: Touchstone (1999).

Manhattan. How and where else, besides Harlem, did these people gather, become friends, rivals and sometimes sworn enemies?

Young's table of contents includes over a dozen writers born or raised in and around Washington, DC: Elizabeth Alexander; Lewis Grandison Alexander; Gwendolyn B. Bennett; Waring Cuney; Clarissa Scott Delany; Joel Dias-Porter; Thomas Sayers Ellis; Julia Fields; Rachel Eliza Griffiths; Charlotte Forten Grimké; Walter Everette Hawkins; Essex Hemphill; Dolores Kendrick.

Sterling Brown's high-school teacher Jessie Fauset was Du Bois's literary editor (perhaps more) at *The Crisis*. Fauset introduced Countée, thirty-five years younger than Du Bois, to his future-father-in-law, to Alain Locke, twenty years Countée's senior. Langston met Bruce Nugent in Washington DC, then introduced Bruce Nugent to Wallie Thurman, who genuinely admired Nugent's line drawings of Harlem dancers, but in any case tended to surround himself with people "more than a trifle insane."[28]

The history of movements is the often parallel history of women working alongside men. Poet Georgia Douglas Johnson's house at 1461 South Street NW in DC became the "S" Street Salon, part literary gathering place, part liar's club, where for forty years the Saturday Nighters would attend her at-homes. Poetry readings and book discussions featured Countée, Alice Dunbar-Nelson, Jessie Fauset, Angelina Weld Grimké, Langston, Locke, Bruce Nugent, Eulalie Spence, Anne Spencer, Toomer, and, of course, Sterling Brown.

The American vernacular of Mark Twain and Jack London, stylistically embraced by Britons like James Wood,[29] is so pervasive in American culture that American's aren't always aware of it. Inseparable from that vernacular are the Great Liars, tellers of tall tales, yarn-spinners, of whom Sterling Brown, like Twain, proudly considered himself one.

As for Zora, she "wasn't just *at* a party," said Sterling Brown not exaggerating by much, "she *was* the party."[30]

"Snob," in the lexicon of Dr. Locke, who tended to dominate the conversation, apparently wasn't a four-letter word.

---

28. Thurman, *Infants of the Spring*, p. 194.

29. See Mencken, H.L. *The American Language.* https://www.gutenberg.org/ebooks/43376.

30. Sterling Brown, quoted in Hemenway, *Zora Neale Hurston*, p. 61.

"Washington," he sniffed, "externally is like a real capital—only it lacks the proper people."

Sometimes, on "S" Street, the conversation was nothing but lies.

"You are years away," Dorothy West lied to Countée, who fretted about getting fat, "from being portly."[31]

She couldn't say the same for Arna.

Sometimes, "S" Street conversation was trash talk, back-talk, TALL smack-talk.

"I have just finished *Madame Bovary*," Langston told Locke, "and think that the best thing Emma did was to kill herself."[32]

"Lang!" Arna was always happy to see him.[33]

"Always something," Langston said, "to keep a writer from writing!"[34]

Wallie ribbed Langston. "Some fun, eh, kid?"[35]

"Know what I thought of?" Zora told Langston, "A Negro art colony. You and Wallie and Aaron and Bruce and me and all our crowd."[36]

"I dug your piece," Arna told Langston, "in *The New Republic*."[37]

"Um-huh! Hey, Arna!" Langston said.[38]

"Yeah, man."[39]

"You wouldn't, by any chance, have a $5 spot would you?"[40]

---

31. Letter from Dorothy West to Countée Cullen dated 6 September 1933, *Where the Wild Grape Grows*, p. 197-98.

32. Letter from Langston Hughes to Alain Locke dated 24 August 1924, p. 39.

33. Routine salutation from *AB-LH* Letters, passim.

34. Letter from Langston Hughes to Arna Bontemps dated April 17, 1943, *Selected Letters of Langston Hughes*, p. 250.

35. Letter from Wallace Thurman to Langston Hughes, dated [July 10, 1934], *Collected Writings of Wallace Thurman*, p. 129.

36. Letter from Zora Neale Hurston to Langston Hughes dated [May 31, 1929], *Zora Neale Hurston: A Life in Letters*, p. 145.

37. *Arna Bontemps-Langston Hughes Letters*, p. 160.

38. Letter from Langston Hughes to Arna Bontemps dated August 30, 1958, *Selected Letters of Langston Hughes*, p. 349.

39. Letter from Arna Bontemps to Langston Hughes dated 24 September 1943. *Arna Bontemps-Langston Hughes Letters*, p. 144.

40. *Arna Bontemps-Langston Hughes Letters*, p. 109.

"I *knowed*," Arna belly-laughed, "they's a ace in that deck somewheres!"[41]

Other times, the conversation got highty-tighty on "S" Street.

"Toomer," Wallie told Langston, "should be enshrined a genius."[42]

"Toomer," Du Bois agreed, praising *Cane*, "has written a powerful book."[43]

Sometimes, in other rooms, behind closed doors, on "S" Street, the conversation, said Sterling Brown, pulling on his pipe, or puffing a Tiparillo cigar, "was quite intellectual/And advanced."[44]

"Alain," Hughes urged Locke.

"Don't be skeerd," Zora teased.[45]

"Do me a grand favor—"[46]

"You need," Hurston butted in, "some money? I'll keep my big mouf shut."[47]

"Mail me $10 until the first when my royalties come due again."[48]

*

The sense of place in a poem like "Harlem Happiness" is as fundamental to Brown's verse as are settings like the Five Points of Atlanta, Gee A, Jeff City, Nashville or Lynchburg. A map of Sterling Brown's world reads like traditional migration routes—Texas and Louisiana, Harlem and North Carolina, the liminality between natural and spirit worlds. In Cajun country, where the nearest cabin

---

41. Letter dated 23 September 1939 from Arna Bontemps to Langston Hughes. *Arna Bontemps–Langston Hughes Letters*, p. 41.

42. Letter from Wallace Thurman to Langston Hughes, c. May-June 1929, *Collected Writings of Wallace Thurman*, p. 119.

43. Quoted in Leonard Harris & Charles Molesworth, *Alain L. Locke: The Biography of a Philosopher*. Chicago: University of Chicago Press (2008), p. 155.

44. "The Last Ride of Wild Bill," Part VI, lines 21-22, p. 149.

45. Letter from Zora Neale Hurston to Langston Hughes dated [winter 1929/30], quoted in Carla Kaplan, *Zora Neale Hurston: A Life in Letters*, p. 158.

46. Letter from Langston Hughes to Alain Locke, January 1927, *Selected Letters of Langston Hughes*, p. 64.

47. Letter from Zora Neale Hurston to Langston Hughes dated [5 September 1929], quoted in Carla Kaplan, ed. *Zora Neale Hurston: A Life in Letters*, p. 149.

48. Letter from Langston Hughes to Alain Locke, January 1927, *Selected Letters of Langston Hughes*, p. 64.

lies twelve miles nigh, we find backwoods doctors attending super-
stitious parishes.

In what might as well be Pittsburgh, poor immigrants, black
and white,

> *burst forth from the factory*
> *When the Abe Lincoln noon–whistle*
> *blasted you free,*
> *For one hot hour;*[49]

In Chicago,

> *the tommy guns drill, and the bodies fall,*
> *. . . folks get killt, no difference at all,*[50]

In the cotton South, down Arkansas,

> *there's hell to pay;*
> *The devil is a rider,*
> *God may be the owner,*
> *But he's rich and forgetful,*
>
> *And far away.*[51]

V A Sense of History

The era Young calls "After the Hurricane" (2009–2020) is one of
violent unrest in the wake of pandemic police-involved shootings of
black women and children. Sad to say, but Sterling Brown's more
topical "protest" poems seem to have aged at least as well if not better
than his classicizing bucolics.

As social turmoil followed cultural change, the Ku Klux Klan re-
surfaced during Ida Mae's early years. The race riots of the nineteen
teens, appropriation of black property, lynchings, burnings at the
stake and other forms of domestic terror were visited upon blacks
and Jews from Atlanta, Brownsville, Chicago, East St. Louis, Hous-
ton, Memphis and Ida Mae's native Tulsa.

---

49. "Side by Side," Part V, lines 2–5, p. 254.
50. "All Are Gay," lines 28–30, p. 224.
51. "Arkansas Chant," lines 12–16, p. 205.

Sterling Brown's *Collected Poems* present overt themes of freedom and justice traditionally associated with survival strategies veiled in the Spirituals. Young's *African American Poetry* also anthologizes half a dozen Sterling Brown poems, none more powerful or timely than "Southern Cop" (1936).

Southern Cop

Let us forgive Ty Kendricks.
The place was Darktown. He was young.
His nerves were jittery. The day was hot.
The Negro ran out of the alley.
And so he shot.

Let us understand Ty Kendricks.
The Negro must have been dangerous,
Because he ran;
And here was a rookie with a chance
To prove himself a man.

Let us condone Ty Kendricks
If we cannot decorate.
When he found what the Negro was running for,
It was too late;
And all we can say for the Negro is
It was unfortunate.

Let us pity Ty Kendricks,
He has been through enough,
Standing there, his big gun smoking,
Rabbit-scared, alone,
Having to hear the wenches wail
And the dying Negro moan.[52]

Women and children cheer on lynchings as if they were sporting events. Moonshine swilled from Coca-Cola bottles is used as lighter fluid on embers beneath what Anne Spencer calls pyred black bodies.

---

52. "Southern Cop," p. 215, lines 1–22.

In "He Was a Man," Brown narrates a lynching that takes place in "broad noon daylight."[53] Not unlike today, yesterday's lynchings weren't exclusively carried out by "Ku Klux hoods."[54]

> *They strung him up on Main Street,*
> *On a tree in the Court House Square,*
> *And people came from miles around*
> *To enjoy a holiday there,*
> *He was a man, and they laid him down.*
>
> *They hung him and they shot him,*
> *They piled packing cases around,*
> *They burnt up Will's black body,*
> *'Cause he shot a white man down;*
> *"He was a man, and we'll lay him down."*
>
> *It wasn't no solemn business,*
> *Was more like a barbecue,*
> *The crackers yelled when the fire blazed,*
> *And the women and the children too—*
> *He was a man, and we laid him down.*
>
> *The Coroner and the Sheriff*
> *Said "Death by Hands Unknown."*[55]

Those who survive being shot in the back feed the relocation-centers of the nation's carceral-industrial complex:

From "All Are Gay"

> *This is the schooling ungrudged by the state.*
> *Short in time, as usual, but fashioned to last.*
> *The scholars are apt, and never play truant.*
> *The stockade is waiting. . . . And they will not be late.*[56]

---

53. "He Was a Man," line 33, p. 162-163.

54. *Ibid.*

55. *Ibid.*

56. "All Are Gay," lines 3–6, p. 224.

From "Convict"

Jim is on the gang,
Working on the road;
Goes out in the morning
With the prison load;

Sees the little shacks
Mist covered, dim. . . .
And another daybreak
Comes back to him,

That brought him to handcuffs,
And a dingy cell,
Daytime on the highways,
Nights in hell.

When the truck rolls back
As the sun goes down,
Jim sees what he is used to
In Shantytown.

Sleeping hounds everywhere,
Flies crawling thick,
Grownups drunken
And children sick.

Three long months
Till he takes his ease,
With their filth and squalor
And miseries. . . .

Jim as the night falls
Gets his view
Of the longed-for heaven
He's returning to. . . .[57]

---

57. "Convict," p. 105.

VI A Sense of Swing

If Sterling Brown's *Collected Poems* were all bull-whips, trace chains and lynchings—if he were a one-note poet—Maya Angelou wouldn't have bothered writing about him.

Some keys to Sterling Brown's work are to be found in folklore, some in his sense of character, others in his sense of place, still others in his sense of history, but most if not all in his highly musical sense of swing.

As early as 1930, Sterling Brown was writing about blues lyrics the way scholars write about the poetry of Bob Dylan. Sterling Brown honors his debt to blues, jazz and gospel as sources of inspiration.

Rappers acknowledge Sterling Brown's pioneering role in the evolution of a Black Aesthetic. *On Rhapsodies in Black: Music and Words from the Harlem Renaissance*, blues singers, Neo-Soul singer-songwriters,[58] rappers, spoken-word performance-artists and tap-dancers cross and re-cross the "seeming divide"[59] between oral and literary traditions, classical and vernacular, gospel and gangsta, high and low. Coolio reads Arna's "Day Breakers;" Ice-T recites Claude McKay's "If We Must Die;" Eartha Kitt enacts, chants, dances, *conjures* a poem by Sterling Brown's contemporary Nicolás Guillén, "Sensemayá—Chant for Killing a Snake," translated by Langston in such a way that the speech, song and dance rhythms he heard behind the Cuban-Spanish original approximate the African-American vernacular. Carl Hancock Rux performs Richard Bruce Nugent's "Smoke, Lilies and Jade."

Brown's poems were influenced in content, form and cadence by black music, including work songs, blues and jazz. Some poems are influenced by spirituals such as you hear on the soundtrack from *O Brother, Where Art Thou?* —"Lonesome Valley," as performed by the Fairfield Four. The Slim Greer series— up-tempo, danceable, somewhere between jazz, blues and boogie-woogie or stride piano— is jauntier.

---

58. https://en.wikipedia.org/wiki/Singer-songwriter

59. Young, Kevin, ed. "The Difficult Miracle." Introduction to *African American Poetry: 250 Years of Struggle & Song*. New York: Library of America (2020), pp. xxxix-lix.

Here, in a perfect combination of scene, characterization, in stride-piano rhythm, Sterling Brown busts a nuttin' toon replete with sexual innuendo. On YouTube, readers can find jump blues or kings-of-jukebox swing musicians like Louis ("Beans and Cornbread") Jordan.

> *An' he started a-tinklin'*
> *Some mo'nful blues,*
> *An' a-pattin' the time*
> *With No. Fourteen shoes.*

You can't just take this blues in by eye; you have to hear it in your head.

Slim Greer, passing for white while romancing a Southern belle, is faced with a potential lynch-mob moment of racial reckoning when she

> *Crept into the parlor*
> *Soft as you please*
> *Where Slim was agitatin'*
> *The ivories.*

> *Heard Slim's music—*
> *An' then, hot damn!*
> *Shouted sharp—"Nigger!"*
> *An' Slim said, "Ma'am?"*[60]

Sterling Brown is a famously fussy orchestrator of transitions; his scores mix a wide range of tonal centers, majors and rippling "minors on de black and yellow keys,"[61] octaves and octaroons, "mournful blues with hill-billy tunes,"[62] block-chords fore-armed like poet Cecil Taylor.

Sterling Brown's verse experiments are as formally varied as his subject matter. Some ballads are based in meter and refrain rather than rhyme. "New St. Louis Blues" is a triptych in triplets, its

---

60. "Slim Greer," lines 49-56, bottom of p. 86, top of p. 87.

61. "Ma Rainey." Part II, line 8, p. 70.

62. "Side by Side, Part VIII, line 2, p. 256.

three sections, "Market Street Woman," "Tornado Blues" and "Low Down" fleshed out in five or six stanzas each.

Steeped as he was in the classical repertoire, Sterling Brown never lets that interfere with his sense of swing.

23 Ms. Annye, Li'l Robert Johnson and Them

Blues All Different Ways

Less blood pooled over juke-joint floors on hot Saturday nights than ink has spilled in the name of "Robert Johnson." He wasn't even born in the Mississippi Delta, didn't always answer to the surname Johnson. Grown folk called him Li'l Robert. He called himself R.L., short for Robert Leroy. How did a "1930s blues singer-guitarist who lived a short and colorful life"[1] become a commemorative postage stamp? By what degrees was he transformed in life from the laughing stock of contemporaries into a "good player of old-time songs,"[2] into a bona fide recording artist and thence in death into "the pre-eminent exponent of the Delta tradition"?[3]

Until recently, we didn't know much about R.L., except that he was a "strange dude."[4] Before Conforth & Wardlow, our understanding of him derived almost entirely from R.L.'s recorded output—104 minutes of music, sixteen original sides, a baker's dozen of alternate takes, twenty-nine songs in total, performed on just two dates, as noted in *Robert Johnson: The Complete Recordings* (Centennial Collection). But a musician's repertoire is just one aspect of her or his career; "records," Elijah Wald reminds us, "are not the whole story."[5]

We knew more about R.L.'s tunings and touring than we did about the bitterness Ms. Anderson and others hear behind his music, the dark crossroads of his inner life, the tears inside. Conforth & Wardlow's evocations of his childhood out beyond the cotton fields, off dusty roads, among the wooden shotgun-shacks of Hazlehurst, stilt-

---

1. Marcus, Greil. "The Devil Had Nothing To Do With It." *New York Review of Books*. (3 December 2020). https://www.nybooks.com/articles/2020/12/03/robert-johnson-devil-nothing-to-do-with-it/

2. Conforth, Bruce, and Gayle Dean Wardlow. *Up Jumped the Devil: The Real Life of Robert Johnson*. Chicago: Chicago Review Press (2019), p. 12.

3. Gioia, Ted. *Music: A Subversive History*. New York: Basic Books (2019).

4. Wald, Elijah. *Escaping the Delta: Robert Johnson & The Invention of the Blues*. New York: Amistad (2004), p. 113.

5. Wald, p. 40.

ed, on raised brick, over flood-prone flatlands, are as vital to R.L.'s music as Ry Cooder's atmospheric slide is to Wim Wenders' *Paris, Texas*.

Half a dozen books peel back layers of fact, truth, half-truth, "exaggerations or outright lies,"[6] none diminishing the man or his music.

How much of R.L.'s life's reflected in his lyrics or vice versa?

> *My poor father died and left me*
> *my poor mother done the best that she could*
> *My poor father died and left me*
> *my poor mother done the best that she could*

We may never know. Born illegitimate, R.L. never knew who his father was till his teens, when he adopted his father's surname, becoming "Robert Johnson." What we know for a fact is that R.L.'s mother had to give him up when he was just an infant. His childhood was divided between the plantations of Mississippi and the city of Memphis, where he was sent to live with his extended family between the ages of two and nine. We can't know how that made him feel—how it made her feel—when he was a boy. At one time or another, it might even have seemed to R.L. that she'd abandoned him. I wonder if it ever seemed that way to her.

Perhaps R.L.'s is the archetypal coming-of-age story of a young man, his adventures and misadventures on the road. Seen another way, the parable of his talents is a cautionary tale of drunkenness and violence. R.L. was a blues traveler, but the major triad of his life consisted of the thirds or fifths of Memphis and West Helena, Arkansas, with Mississippi at the root.

Since there are as many ways to retell R.L.'s life story as there are ways to cover his songs, biographers should get creative with the storytelling but not the facts. Some R.L. stories ring true. Others don't add up. Did he really hit a lick or strum a chord in the graveyard at midnight? Sure. Lots of players did that. On the other hand, R.L.'s "Preachin' Blues" never even mentions the Devil. Its subtitle, "Up Jumped the Devil," wasn't even R.L.'s idea. No PR is bad PR. R.L.'s record producers simply used a marketing gimmick to cash in on the success of R.L. predecessors like Peetie Wheatstraw, who alternate-

---

6. Conforth & Wardlow 253.

ly dubbed himself the "High Sheriff from Hell" or the "Devil's Son-in-Law." Who's ultimately responsible for the legend that R.L., in a Faustian bargain, down at the crossroads, sold his soul to the Devil at midnight in exchange for supernatural skills? The Devil, probably.

On the other hand, Sterling Brown would not dismiss as mere "folklore" the survival of Yoruba and other West African belief systems among black transplants in Brazil, Cuba, the Delta, Haiti or Louisiana, folktales of New Negroes in a New World, so embarrassing to scholars, so fascinating to music lovers.

Lead Belly, Blind Lemon Jefferson and Blind Willie Johnson were among the countless blues musicians playing for passing change on sidewalks and street corners when R.L. was born. In New Orleans, white and black music—Cajun, Caribbean, Creole, Dixieland, white hymns—got gumboed together. Later for "reasons," Wald writes, "cultural and commercial rather than musical,"[7] bluegrass versus blues, guitars and harmonicas versus banjos and fiddles, Nashville country versus Memphis gospel and jazz—all these beautiful strains of American music you hear re-blended on a soundtrack like *O Brother, Where Art Thou?* began to self-segregate.

"Johnson's vision of the blues is more indebted to the phonograph than to the plantation," Ted Gioia writes, and is "as much a reflection of commercial tastes as the continuation of a folkloric tradition."[8] Muddy Waters remembered several equally good players, ones who never got recorded. By Wald's estimate, for every R.L. there were thousands if not tens of thousands of blues players who simply never made it to the recording studio, much less the big time. R.L. seems emblematic of the commercial viability of essentially folk art in an age of mechanical reproduction.[9]

As for Delta blues in particular, B.B. King reminds us that though scholars and record producers zealously categorize blues into distinct styles, Piedmont or West Coast, when King was growing up in Mississippi his own boyhood idols were not from the Delta at all, but rather Texas and Louisiana. The term "Delta"—Upper Delta, Lower

7. *Escaping the Delta*, p. 194.

8. Gioia, Ted. *Delta Blues: The Life and Times of the Mississippi Masters Who Revolutionized American Music.* New York: W.W. Norton (2008), p. 169.

9. Gerald Early argues that "the Harlem Renaissance, which was largely a kind of entertainment-based movement when one considers its musical and stage connections, would not have been possible" otherwise. Early 34.

Delta—is one that covers a vast area (the Arkansas-Mississippi Delta, "cotton-field" or "urban" styles) that doesn't always recognize hard and fast distinctions.

When R.L. was a boy, mainstream white records were produced by whites for white consumption. Then the "race-record," produced by whites for black consumption, was born. But when we talk race-records what we're really talking about is economic disparity. 78s existed to sell phonographs, bigger-ticket items sold in furniture stores most blacks couldn't afford. But the 78s themselves were sold at five-and-dime stores that blacks did patronize. The juke joint was sharing stage with the juke box. Though not the first so-called race records (those of Mamie Smith, Ethel Waters and Alberta Hunter preceded her), the Bessie Smith recordings that date from when R.L. was about twelve precede the first Rolling Stones album by just forty years. OK Records had no clue Mamie Smith's "Crazy Blues" would sell 75,000 copies in a single month. Neither did Columbia Records expect *Robert Johnson: The Complete Recordings* (1990) to sell hundreds of thousands during its first several weeks of release, more than fifty million to date.

Before getting sidetracked into debates about "black music for white people," let's put this into perspective. As for blues in general, up the Mississippi from New Orleans the Memphis of R.L.'s childhood was a river port with all the corruption that still implies. Her cops were crooked as the Delta. Frank Stokes' "Mr. Crump Don't Like It" is wonderfully evocative of what R.L. heard while running wild in the streets. The blues was no more welcome in respectable homes like that of R.L.'s mother, who sang in church, than rap/hip-hop was in houses I grew up in.

"Child, I swear 'fore God," Ida Mae said, "you play that zigaboo mess up hyeah in this howse, I beatchoo half ta deaf!"

Gioia's *Music: A Subversive History* is partly concerned with the role of class and caste in musical innovation, with how, whether tango or flamenco, "breakthroughs in music almost always come from outsiders and the underclass—slaves, bohemians, rebels."[10] Peasant virtues, E. Franklin Frazier reminds us in *Black Bourgeoisie* (1957), are middle-class faults.[11]

---

10. Gioia, Ted. *Music: A Subversive History*. New York: Basic Books (2019).

11. E. Franklin Frazier, "Durham: Capital of the Black Middle Class," quoted

Why on earth would the god-fearing celebrate on Sundays dev-il-music which sang the life it lived on Saturdays around the saw mills and lumber camps, about sloe gin, fast women and razor fights? Blues guitarist B.B. King testifies he was not always welcome as accompanist for gospel singers. "The blues always dance," Young says, "cheek to cheek with a church."[12]

Until 1960, R.L. was known primarily to 78-rpm. record col-lectors like Wardlow, and/or was meticulously archived in private collections by cognoscenti like cartoonist Robert Crumb, of the *Heroes of Blues, Jazz & Country* series. African-American audiences didn't rescue Lightnin' Hopkins, Mississippi John Hurt, Skip James or Booker T. Washington ("Bukka") White from obscurity. The most-ly-white blues revivalists did. Before Woodstock (1969) how many African-American radio stations were claiming Jimi Hendrix as their own? Can the boutique black publishing imprints of corporate conglomerates or periodicals take credit for the strong resurgence of African-American writing today?

There's a more tolerant way to view this. Think of Little Walter's Chicago sound as amplified Delta blues; think how blues influenced British skiffle music, which became the British Invasion. Two Brit-ish expatriates, long since inducted into the Country Music Hall of Fame, were responsible for the 1936 San Antonio session by which "Robert Johnson" became known to the rest of America and Britain. It was the release of *King of the Delta Blues Singers* (1961) that brought his artistry to that new generation of artists born around World War II, who in turn revolutionized rock in particular and pop in general.

Peter Guralnick's *Looking to Get Lost: Adventures in Music and Writing* is informative about the influence of R.L.'s music on Eric Clapton and others a generation before the first Columbia boxed set appeared in 1990. Today, R.L. is perhaps without exaggeration your favorite gui-tarist's favorite guitarist. When Wald talks about the "blues revival," what he's really talking about is the mass commercial distribution to a relatively affluent post-urban white audience of an essentially black folk art pioneered by a handful of recorded blues players and sing-ers, Delta or otherwise—like Muddy Waters, left scratching his head

in *The New Negro*, p. 333.

12. Young, Kevin. "Money Road." Quoted in *African American Poetry: 250 Years of Struggle & Song.* New York: Library of America (2020), lines 11-12, p. 914.

about "how these white kids were playing the blues my black kids was bypassing."[13] Perhaps black folk simply moved on from down-home, country-blues music the way listeners of my generation moved on from "dinosaur rock."

Call it cross-over or whatever, the pop I grew up on as I split a decade of formative years in San Francisco and its Silicon Valley suburbs between 1969 and 1985, seems enormously sophisticated now, though I couldn't hear it that way then. And already it had re-miscegenated to the point where The Swampers, five good ol' boys outta Muscle Shoals, Alabama, formed those Stax and Atlantic Records rhythm sections backing some of the most iconic soul music in American history: Aretha Franklin on "I Never Loved a Man" (1967) or The Staple Singers on "I'll Take You There" (1972). Listening to Phoebe Snow sing "Harpo's Blues" (1973), I still can't tell which accompaniment swings more authentically, pianist Teddy Wilson's blue-veined white delicacy or tenor Zoot Sims' black saxophone spit.

*

Preserving folk tradition is by definition what griot elders do. One griot woman, Annye C. Anderson, was named Annie Clara at birth. *Brother Robert: Growing Up with Robert Johnson* is her as-told-to memoir, co-authored by Preston Lauterbach with a foreword by Elijah Wald, of Ms. Anderson's memories, dictated eighty years after Robert Leroy's death, of her life from the time she was a young girl during the Great Depression till the day when, at twelve, she heard the news.

"Li'l Robert, he dead."[14]

R.L. was twenty-seven.

Up Jumped the Devil: The Real Life of Robert Johnson is a scholarly account of R.L.'s life by Rock & Roll Hall of Fame ex-curator and ethnomusicologist Bruce Conforth and fellow blues historian Gayle Dean Wardlow. It complements but does not supplant *Brother Robert*. Because oral history is just one component of *Up Jumped the Devil*. Whereas *Brother Robert* is the oral history of an oral historian. The ancestral grain of Ms. Anderson's voice—orality, Lauterbach's showing of Ms. Anderson's telling—is as much what that book, and the

---

13. *Escaping the Delta*, p. 247.

14. Bruce Conforth and Gayle Dean Wardlow. *Up Jumped the Devil: The Real Life of Robert Johnson*. Chicago: Chicago Review Press (2019).

book you're now reading, is about as it is the life of Robert Johnson himself.

The Memphis blues W.C. Handy was standardizing the year before R.L. was born, the music R.L. grew up hearing live as he followed his working mother from plantation to plantation, was the music sharecroppers listened to after work in the rice fields and soybean fields around Robinsonville, or Clarksdale. Without electricity or radios, ex-slaves who'd never ventured beyond the region and were curious to hear travel-tales sung by itinerant blues players depended on live music for entertainment. Country dances were always staged on Saturday nights with a musician providing the music.

Though Son House "learned him stuff,"[15] by that time R.L. was already so good that people came from miles away to hear him play parties, fish fries, picnics and jukes. Later, he began writing his own songs. Acquired a distaste for working cotton fields. The boogie was *in* him, and had—though he endured beatings from well-meaning custodial adults for refusing work—to get out.

When R.L. discovered his teenaged bride was "percolatin'," he tried to do the decent thing: married, settled down to farming by day, playing music nights and weekends. Once his child bride and newborn both died in childbirth while he was out playing the dances, R.L. never again attempted to settle down. Why should he kill himself carrying an 11-foot, heavy canvas sack full of cotton for \$.50 a day? Memphis, where cops got bribed, dice got shot, and street-walkers cost as little as \$.50 apiece, came to know R.L. well.

Li'l Robert grabbed up his ticking bag, took off down the road, down those lonesome blue highways, US Route 41, Highway 61, from Beale Street to New Orleans and back, carrying his guitar and his dirty laundry, crashing at the houses of extended family members, for a day or two, just long enough to scarf a few square meals and get him a hot bath, and then—sometimes without so much as a thank-you or a goodbye—went back out on the road. As for women, he loved them "like a hobo loves a train—off one and on another."[16]

"He played on the streets during the day, in local jukes in the evening, and when they closed, unless he had a better offer, he would

---

15. Conforth & Wardlow 74.

16. Conforth & Wardlow 230.

play on the nearby plantations. There was no closing time for a juke at a plantation, especially on weekends."[17]

A barrelhouse, or juke joint, was part speakeasy, part dance-club, part bordello, part flophouse. Sometimes, a musician's take was all she could drink, plus $5. On a good night, tips for playing requests upped the ante to $25. Wasn't like they had hotel rooms booked in advance. Singer-guitarist Johnny Shines said sometimes they didn't even know where the next meal was coming from. Under the best of circumstances, a Saturday night juke joint was as dangerous as a house party or club in its inner-city equivalent. When I lived in Harlem, off-duty New York Police Department cops moonlighting as bouncers at night spots or house parties to pay off predatory mortgages in the bad neighborhoods of Long Island—Baldwin, Freeport—used to joke that the better the music, the more likely you were to get shot.

If we think blues in terms of regional centers instead of regional styles—Clarksdale, heart of the Mississippi Delta; West Helena, heart of the Arkansas Delta, and Memphis—all that running back and forth R.L. did makes perfect sense. Mississippi was still a dry state and liquor came across the river from Arkansas. For R.L., the area between Memphis, Robinsonville, Mississippi (forty miles south) and West Helena, Arkansas—a gigging bluesman's cash cow—was indeed a Devil's triangle.

What R.L. played really just depended on where he was playing. In Chicago, R.L. met Memphis Minnie, Roosevelt Sykes, Big Joe Williams, and Washboard Sam, each active on the South Side at one time or another. In rural Illinois, where the locals had never seen a black man before, R.L. performed as a kind of freak-show act, and might play a square dance. In black-bottom Detroit, on his way up into Canada, he might play a river-front baptism or the local gospel-radio show. In Jersey, where Sinatra was launched into stardom headlining the Hoboken Four, R.L. might play 6/8 tarantellas at Italian weddings, polkas, klezmer music or plain old waltzes in 3/4 time. Harlem and New York City might mean the big time—seven million inhabitants patronizing hundreds of clubs and speakeasies, radio stations and theaters, professional sports and arts venues, Maria Callas performing *Madame Butterfly*. Gioia says, no "traditional

---

17. Conforth & Wardlow 249.

blues singer has ever sold more recordings or appealed to a broader slice of the public than Robert Johnson."[18]

The gulf between R.L.'s biography and discography was impassable until I approached the latter from the former. I was born in what Conforth & Wardlow call the Upper South. Kansas City was a blues hub better known for shouters like Big Joe Turner than for crooners like Robert Johnson. The pre-Depression Memphis world Ms. Anderson narrates survived intact until the early 1970s, the time of my own upbringing, with its Sunday brunches of calf's brains and scrambled eggs, smack-talking relatives seated on folding chairs, slamming dominoes down on portable card tables, snacking on pickled pigs feet and pork rinds with plenty hot sauce. Sunday dinner might be the whole hog roasting on a backyard spit, with sides of collard greens, skillet corn bread, red beans and rice; might be that fecal funk of chittlins soaking somewhere in bathtub bleach. So much of what Ms. Anderson recalls about caste, class, music and religion I took for granted.

In the late 1960s and early 1970s, my family summers during school vacation were spent driving cross-country in eight-cylinder, four-door sedans choked with Green-Book food. We visited family after family after family throughout what Conforth & Wardlow call "the Lower South"—Oklahoma, the Ozarks—as well as the Rockies of Colorado, beneath wide Wyoming skies, through Nevada into Arizona and on to California, then back again through flatlands of Kansas, Nebraska, and on down, across miles and miles of Texas, through bayous of Louisiana. Always and everywhere, on reel-to-reel tape decks, on vinyl, on 8-track tapes, music marked my entire adolescence: work songs, field hollers, blues. These soundscapes were so much a part of my childhood that it took decades of distance to hear these musics fresh.

In the context of R.L.'s ubiquity, the Grateful Dead lyrics from "Truckin',"[19,20] (1970) about a band on the road, don't seem at all "trippy," in the psychedelic sense:

---

18. Gioia, Ted. *Delta Blues: The Life and Times of the Mississippi Masters Who Revolutionized American Music*. New York: W.W. Norton (2008), p. 175.

19. Quoted at https://www.dead.net/lyricsby/robert-hunter.

20. See http://artsites.ucsc.edu/gdead/AGDL/copyrigh.html

Arrows of neon and flashing marquees out on Main Street
Chicago, New York, Detroit and it's all on the same street
Your typical city involved in a typical daydream
Hang it up and see what tomorrow brings

Dallas, got a soft machine
Houston, too close to New Orleans
New York got the ways and means
But just won't let you be

What in the world ever became of sweet Jane?
She lost her sparkle, you know she isn't the same
Livin' on reds, vitamin C, and cocaine
All a friend can say is, "Ain't it a shame?"

Truckin', up to Buffalo
Been thinkin', you got to mellow slow
It takes time, you pick a place to go
And just keep truckin' on

Busted, down on Bourbon Street
Set up, like a bowlin' pin
Knocked down, it gets to wearin' thin
They just won't let you be

You're sick of hangin' around and you'd like to travel
Get tired of travelin', you want to settle down
I guess they can't revoke your soul for tryin'
Get out of the door and light out and look all around

Truckin', I'm a goin' home
Whoa, whoa, baby, back where I belong
Back home, sit down and patch my bones
And get back truckin' on

But R.L. had bigger ambitions than just performing live. A hit record would mean he could command higher takes at the jukes, and a wider reputation among women. So, he borrowed him a Borsalino hat, a pinstripe suit, had his picture taken on Beale Street, had his cap-toed shoes shined up sharp as his knees, held up his high-mile-age Gibson L–l guitar, its fretboard stripped near-clean above the sound-hole. One Saturday morning R.L. hitched a ride with a white couple, the whites riding behind like Ms. Daisy with R.L. at the wheel (so as not to 'rouse suspicion, y'unnerstand). R.L. drove three days and 700 Texas miles from Memphis, by way of Mississippi and Louisiana. Ya see, he was headed way over in San Antone; make him some reckids; maybe git famous; somethin' you might call, like dat dere, a recordin' artist.

R.L. was twenty-five.

Without a word of warning, Old Devil Blues met R.L. in some juke joint on a hot Saturday night. There was hell to pay for the life he'd led. R.L. had his share of the bad luck and trouble blues musicians traditionally sing. He'd lost two wives and two children. Night before that first recording session in San Antonio, he was arrested, beaten, thrown in jail, his guitar busted all to pieces. Then he was bailed out, just in time for his 10 a.m. recording session, borrowed (legend has it) a guitar and laid down 8-tracks from 10 till late. R.L. got run over by a truck; another guitar burnt up in a fire. He died the year Weldon Johnson and Bessie Smith were both killed in car accidents.

The cause of death listed on his certificate is "no doctor." But, really, all the doctors in Mississippi couldn't have helped him none. Lethal admixtures of women, corn whiskey (from which R.L. developed internal bleeding) and geography spelled The End. There was no sheriff's investigation, no coroner's inquest, no autopsy. Locals shrugged off the news of yet another rambling juker's death in a place where rowdy patrons drank, danced, shot dice and hooked up for casual sex the way Memphis might shrug off the news of yet another rapper shot in the club. 1938, August, somewhere around the 16th.

Was R.L. murdered by one the many jealous husbands who caught him messing around with their wives? Some jilted woman get her a mojo hand, hoodoo the hoodoo man? Was R.L. poisoned, shot, bled out by straight-razor? Did he simply die of pneumonia? Mason jars full of moonshine corn-liquor spiked with mothballs were routinely slipped to the unwitting, like a mickey. Hindsight suggests involuntary manslaughter; but such a naphthalin agent, in combination with the ulcerated GI tract in R.L.'s already enlarged lower esophagus, the tears inside, could internally have bled him out, in acute agony, crawling round the floor, over a period of days, howling like the wolf.

. . . stuff I got'll bust your brains out / baby, it'll make you lose your mind

Short shovel, hot day, deep grave dug in that hard Mississippi "gumbo dirt." R.L.'s tarantula-fingers, same day he died, were wrapped in linen, along with the rest of his corpse. A jack-leg, one of those unpaid itinerant preachers like you hear on Reverend Wilkins' "Prodigal Son," ones who took their fee out in trade for food or drink, officiated as they nailed shut that wooden box. R.L. was lain, six feets in the ground, somewhere near Greenwood.

In Boston or Cambridge, in jazz clubs like Scullers, at blues clubs advertised in *The Phoenix*, Ms. Anderson discovered a nightlife forbidden during her "strick" upbringing as a girl in Memphis. As griot elders will, she sought out players who remembered R.L. personally—James, Willie Dixon, John Lee Hooker, Big Walter Horton, Albert King, Sunnyland Slim, Hubert Sumlin. Others, young whites whom Ms. Anderson fully credits for the blues revival—Paul Butterfield, Mick Fleetwood, Lynyrd Skynyrd, Bonnie Raitt, the Steve Miller Band, Johnny Winter—now knew "Robert Johnson" only by name.

The story of L'il Robert has been written and rewritten countless times since his death. Ms. Anderson's story has finally been told in her own words for the first time.

*

In *Escaping the Delta: Robert Johnson & The Invention of the Blues*, Elijah Wald doesn't even attempt a scholarly interpretation of the meaning of the blues. Which is the virtue of his approach, not its failing. Some readers will care more about how Robert Johnson's music works— here Conforth thinks Wald superb—than about what certain unambiguous lyrics mean.

In R.L.'s day, many members of his rural audiences probably could not read lyrics. Though he took music lessons in Memphis, we don't really know whether or how easily R.L. could sight-read music. Triad structure and repetition, Lydia Davis writes, are mnemonic devices common to oral cultures in transition. Blues storytelling conveys maximalist humor, pathos and bottomless depths of folk wisdom with minimalist economy: a powerful few chords, two almost identical opening lines, each paused in the middle, followed by a third turnaround line. Like "Buddy Brown's Blues," by R.L.'s almost exact contemporary Lightnin' Hopkins.

> *I'm gonna get up in the morning / Do like Buddy Brown*
> *I'm gonna get up in the morning / Do like Buddy Brown*
> *Yeah, I'm gon' eat my breakfast / Man, I'm gon' lay back down*

Throw in Southern idiomatic expressions you haven't heard in fifty years, metaphors and similes, a pinch of double-entendre and sexual innuendo. Hudson Whittaker (born Hudson Woodbridge, aka Tampa Red, a Chicago blues musician) says, "she crazy about it / 'cause it fit just right"); and there you have it: a blues verse.

"It don't take but five verses," Big Bill Broonzy explains, "to make a blues."[21]

"Musical language," says Robert Palmer in *Deep Blues*, "expresses, in a way words cannot, something profoundly important about the depth, vitality, and continuity of . . . culture."[22] Sometimes the greatest moments of so-called deep blues are moments of wordless utterance, when a self-accompanied singer lays out, just moans, and rhythmically taps her foot.

As a young writer in search of a voice, I could relate to R.L.'s quest to master his instrument. At age twenty-seven, I went from absorbing music subconsciously to wanting consciously to write about musicians like R.L. Wald won a Grammy for liner-notes, and is, like Peter Guralnick, an exemplar of what sinkholes to avoid in music criticism. Robert Palmer is instructive on that mush-mouthed delivery[23] of Sonny Boy Williamson II, who sings as though he's left his dentures steeping in a studio bar-glass. Palmer is felicitous on the "uniquely orchestral style"[24] Williamson brings to the blues harmonica. A carefully musical writer thinks of words as notes and sequencing; overdubs sentences, paragraphs, essays or even entire books of essays with allusional overtones—voicings and grace notes; gives care-

---

21. *Escaping the Delta*, p. 146.

22. Palmer, Robert. *Deep Blues*, p. 19.

23. *Ibid.*

24. *Ibid.*

ful thought to turnarounds at the ends of sections, chapters; knows how to perform but also transform a piece; how to use sound-associations to make one thing resemble another—the way R.L. suggests a ukulele in the endnotes of "Malted Milk," a tune noted for its jazz feel; the way R.L. Burnside suggests a gallop of horseshoes by drumming his nails on the body of his wooden guitar on "Skinny Woman"; the way Robert Leroy himself imitates a hobo-train chugging along like a steam-engine locomotive on those "Last Fair Deal Gone Down" bass strings; the way R.L. might peal a bell using harmonics on his guitar string; or how R.L.'s slide "shimmers," with a single note, "the leaves tremblin' on the tree."[25] Like a guitarist, a skillful writer will sense when to bottleneck that riff or when to let her naked fingers feather goose-bumps up and down the listener's neck; when to add a verbal fillip, as R.L. does on those last four notes of "Stop Breakin' Down," and when to hold back; will use rubato—quickening or slackening the pace—instead of playing a piece metronomically, with what Wald calls "antiseptic exactitude."[26] What makes a literary piece endlessly listenable is a writer who knows when to whisper, when to shout; when to play it safe and when to take chances; how to make adjustments for both timing and timbre; how much tremolo to shake on that slide chord; knows when to be concise and when expansive; R.L. recorded just two sessions before he died; hadn't yet learned how to sustain inspiration over the course of the half-dozen alternate takes a writer calls drafts/revisions; R.L.'s "Come On In My Kitchen," so trance-like on that first take, is by the second take, Wald says, void of magic; how a writer says essentially similar things in utterly novel ways; how effectively to counterpoint, their melodic lines picked out and their accompanying chord changes strummed, the main points and subpoints a writer is trying to make; how in "Dead Shrimp Blues" R.L. creates the illusion, convincing even to other guitarists, of two players jamming simultaneously, one on bass and the other playing melodies and chords; how to expand one's own tonal range by sometimes resorting to understatement and other times indulging hyperbole; R.L. could play fast, as we hear on "Preachin' Blues (Up Jumped the Devil)," which Wald says is one of

25. Johnson, Robert. "Hell Hound On My Trail." *Robert Johnson: The Centennial Collection*. Legacy Recordings (2011).

26. Wald, Elijah. *Escaping the Delta: Robert Johnson & The Invention of the Blues*. New York: Amistad (2004), p. 134.

R.L.'s wildest and most exciting performances; but among the first things a young writer forgets, and later has to relearn in the progression from virtuosity and back to almost child-like simplicity again, is that chops is as much about executing clean break-outs as it is of digital dexterity at high tempos, or what Conforth & Wardlow call "guitar gymnastics."[27] Ultimately, what a writer needs to learn is when, as Miles learned Coltrane, to "take the harn outcha mouf."[28]

Blues come all different ways. There's blues to boogie, blues for screamin' and cryin':

> *You don't know what love is*
> *'Till you've learned the meaning of the blues*
> *Until you've loved a love you've had to lose,*
> *You don't know what love is.*

There's gallows-humor blues for chain gangs, sitting around the Big House floor, killing hard time.

> *Lord, if you can't send me a woman*
> *please send me a sissy man.*

R.L.'s hero Leroy Carr recorded a drunkard's anthem, "Corn Licker Blues."

> *Now I love my good corn liquor and I really mean I do*
> *Now I love my good corn liquor and I really mean I do*
> *Now I don't care who knows it and I really mean that too*

> *Now I've been drinking my good corn liquor, I mean don't no one get rough*
> *Now I've been drinking my good corn liquor, I mean don't no one get rough*
> *Now I try to treat everybody right but I mean don't start no stuff*

Now "that's," Son House said during a Newport Festival interview, "the blues—B-L-U-S-E."

*

27. Conforth & Wardlow 101.

28. https://life-on-purpose.blog/2018/02/18/take-the-horn-out-of-your-mouth/

As family histories will, R.L.'s gets depressingly familiar and ugly. During R.L.'s lifetime, few of his records sold well, compared to the five or ten thousand copies "Terraplane Blues" had sold, and certainly in comparison with the Columbia releases. Until *King of the Delta Blues Singers*, Robert Johnson was remembered by few locals, some blues contemporaries and what Wald calls "a handful of white folk and jazz fans."[29] Tales got taller. Memories got hazier. Brother Robert's guitar got pawned, never to be redeemed. "Money grabbers,"[30] as Ms. Anderson calls Stephen C. La Vere, acquired rights to the multi-million dollar R.L. estate for a proverbial song. Ethnomusicologist Alan Lomax went down to the Delta, recorded blues artists like David "Honeyboy" Edwards for the Library of Congress. But it was backstage impresarios like John H. Hammond, who kicked R.L.'s posthumous career into high gear.

Was R.L., like Ray Charles, a brilliant synthesizer, a cover-artist skilled at adapting others' melodies or songs and making them his own? Or was he an originator from whom much was stolen and too little credit given? If the latter, wherein does his originality consist?

As instrumentalist, R.L.'s playing style ranged from that of a blues picker influenced by Scrapper Blackwell and others to a one-man rhythm section. He had, some say, eidetic memory; maybe couldn't read music, but had only to see A-natural played just once, or watch a basic C position finger-picked, or see Johnnie Temple tune his own guitar to open E-minor to commit these things to memory. Take that signature, hard-charging boogie beat, what Wald calls the "surprisingly effective trick"[31] of a slide riff on the 1st through 3rd bass-strings (E, B, G) against triplets on 4th, 5th string and 6th strings (D, A, E). Since R.L. recorded "I Believe I'll Dust My Broom" or "Sweet Home Chicago," many juke box heroes have used it to dance-able effect.

Let's sidestep the question of whether or not it was first recorded by Johnnie Temple on "Lead Pencil Blues" in 1935 but was still a novelty when R.L. recorded it later, forget about whether R.L. really invented it any more than Colonel Sanders invented Kentucky Fried

---

29. Wald 188.

30. Anderson, Annye C. with Preston Lauterbach. Foreword by Elijah Wald, *Brother Robert: Growing Up with Robert Johnson*. New York: Hachette Books (2020).

31. *Escaping the Delta*, p. 151.

Chicken. The better question might be where did Johnnie Temple himself learn it? From some other player out in the jukes, one who didn't get into the studio first? The point is that R.L.'s using the bass strings to imitate the left-hand of a barrelhouse pianist had an effect on contemporary guitarists like Robert Lockwood, Jr. in 1937 or 1938 that seems akin to the effect Glenn Gould had on the classical recording world of 1955 when Gould played the piano as if it were a harpsichord. R.L., Lockwood says, "played the guitar like you played the piano."[32]

Tunings can get technical—open-tuned bottleneck, standard-tuned straight blues—even for guitarists, much less non-musicians like me. Until guitarist Rory Block tinkered with "Ramblin' On My Mind," and hit upon a solution confirmed by computer analysis, even Clapton couldn't figure it out. Too time-consuming to change between individual songs, R.L. would change them between sets, often turning his back to the audience to keep them secret. Which brings us to the cross-roads. Wizardry is perhaps a better word than devilry for how R.L.'s art struck contemporaries.

As for the originality of R.L.'s songwriting, the question of which blues, like "32–20" are covers and which original compositions I leave to musicians. No published lyrics or sheet music survives the 78 sessions. So many blues, like those you hear on the 2011 centennial reissue of *Robert Johnson: The Complete Recordings* are reworkings of traditional tunes passed down from musician to musician, often with no originator credited. The matter of who stole what from whom I leave to intellectual property attorneys. But this much seems clear. His sole recording sessions, the first in San Antonio and the last in Dallas, were work-for-hire gigs payed at a flat rate. R.L. owned no rights to his masters, received no royalties. It was a Faustian bargain: either sign a royalty contract from which, if it ever recouped the production costs, he could hypothetically earn $0.25 for each disc sold on a pressing of 10,000 copies; or take $300 or so in cash for just under thirty songs—more money, during the Great Depression, than he'd ever had in hand at any one time. R.L. took the fast money.

Some complain that on vocals, R.L.'s alternate takes—even when they slow down or speed up the tempo—stick too closely to the orig-

---

32. Conforth & Wardlow 191.

inals. Casual listeners are perhaps better served not listening to all twenty-nine tracks from the two-CD set, session after session, originals and alternate takes, back to back sequentially. That can make R.L.'s output seem less varied than it really is. Gioia is struck by the versatility of these twenty-nine songs. But they represent a fraction of the popular tunes he could play by ear or make up on the spur of the moment. R.L. hoped the San Antonio sessions would be the big break he was looking for. Given this rigid 78 formula of three-minute sides—the A-side up-tempo, the B-side a slow number—Conforth & Wardlow prefer to see R.L.'s careful studio takes in a pre-splice era of recording history as consistent rather than lacking adventurousness, a "codifying of his material."[33] No wonder R.L. played it safe, planning out "every word, note, and nuance."[34] "Johnson was one of the most carefully calculated singers," Wald writes, "in blues."[35] Charley Patton routinely aped and clowned for twenty-minute live versions of what we have on record. Think of a song from that first Allman Brothers Band album, "Dreams" or "In Memory of Elizabeth Reed," both stretched out to 19:30 or more on *Live at Sony Brook*. For all we know, the Robert Johnson we hear on record might have been a fundamentally different performer live.

Returning to the controversy of whether R.L. was not just an innovator but an originator, not a cover-artist slapping together pastiches of hit tunes, originalists argue that the genius of Robert Johnson went well beyond knowing which songs to cover. Wald writes that R.L. rewrote hit songs like Hambone Willie Newbern's "Rollin' and Tumblin'," on which he based "Traveling Riverside Blues." R.L. changed up the tempos, added riffs, capoed his guitar to match his singing voice. The beginnings, middles and endings were all carefully worked out. R.L.'s recordings were unlike anything previously heard on juke box. Was R.L. a synthesizer or an originator? Wald argues the former, Conforth & Wardlow the latter. "His songs, his tunings, his playing style were all his: he owned them."[36]

---

33. Conforth & Wardlow, p. 162.

34. Conforth & Wardlow, p. 215.

35. *Escaping the Delta*, p. 141.

36. Conforth & Wardlow, p. 226.

24 The Collective Dark: James Baldwin III

My commitment to writing consists of what translator Raymond N. MacKenzie calls "a clear-sightedness that is almost but not quite cynicism."[1] I suffer no delusions about the "searing hatred" Claude McKay said "only kin can for feel for kin."[2] This is what cemented my relationship with Ida Mae in the final year of her life. In her unsentimental way, she saw my ambition for what it was: incorrigible; unagented.

She had no use for hangers-on. What she did need was a fresh set of eyes to help with all the unglamorous and never-ending chores entailed in tending a literary estate—copyrights, correspondence, reprints, theatrical productions, the preservation, orderly disposition and archiving of cultural artifacts and scholarly materials with various institutional collections. Which meant you met actors you'd grown up watching on television shows like *Gunsmoke* or *Star Trek*, met archivists, arts patrons, bandleaders, musicians, political leaders, religious leaders, set designers, visual artists and others. Ida Mae could and did make introductions, effortlessly.

On 1 June 1985, I arrived in New York—not for the first time, not for good but for a good long while—almost twenty-two years. The subway cars, smothered in graffiti, were not air-conditioned. Rats patrolled the platforms fearlessly, unlike the transit cops. Times Square, before the great Giuliani clean-up transformed it into a family-friendly theme park, was an open-air brothel infested by drug users like the one I soon became.

I was twenty-four.

The *Times Literary Supplement* called me in San Francisco, assigning me to review New Zealand author Janet Frame's *Owls Do Cry*. I read every book of fiction Frame had published up to and including 1984. Then, in time-honored fashion, I bought a one-way ticket to New York. Hit the ground running.

I can't honestly say I moved to New York to keep Ida Mae company during the short remainder of her long life. It just worked out

---

1. Balzac, Honoré de: *Lost Illusions*, Raymond MacKenzie, trans., p. xv.

2. McKay, Claude. "Mulatto", quoted in *The Harlem Renaissance: Hub of African-American Culture, 1920-1930*. New York: Pantheon (1995), p. 34.

that way. Her arthritis smelled like liniment. Eighty-five-years old, Ida Mae had cultural capital but low energy. I had high energy but no capital. Written communication skills might prove useful to her in accomplishing tasks she no longer could or cared to do. I hadn't yet flunked out of Columbia University. But no college degree was required, just basic arithmetic. Between June 1985 and May 1986, we forged a wary alliance.

With no basic training or orientation, I am put to work.

The phone rings.

"Don't just sit there," she grins. "Answer it, child."

I lift the receiver.

"Ida Mae?"

"No, sir," I bumble. "I mean yes, sir. This is the Ida Cullen-Cooper residence. Sir. May I ask who's calling?"

We were a conglomerate of two: Ida Mae was chief executive; I yearned for subordinates of my own to boss around and supervise.

Ida Mae had these gestures. When quashing a motion I'd argue at our board meetings, she'd lower her eyelids, turn her high forehead the other direction, and with those long fingers that curled up backward at the tips (like mine), slowly wave her hand downward, as if closing the trash bin, or a window to keep Midtown soot and dust from griming household surfaces. Or wave her hand sideways, as if brushing crumbs off the bed. Or away from her face, as if shooing a gnat. Or she'd push the thought from her mind, effectively closing the door on it.

Even before microcassette answering machines and caller ID, she always seemed to know who was on the other line, and what they wanted. I never knew. It might be a reporter; might be one of Countée's former students; might be the building superintendent; might be professor so and so from such and such a University, requesting an interview; or it might be the doctor's office.

She'd waive off the call, head off to the bedroom, and close her door.

"She's unavailable at the moment. May I take a message?"

For Ida Mae, New York energy had been electrifying in the 1930s. By the mid-1980s, she was sick; and tired of the place; tired of outrageous supermarket prices; tired of literary events; tired of her part-time housekeeper's foolish chatter; tired of Life. All her friends were dying.

I assume the Reverend Cullen had paid Ida Mae to work as church secretary at Salem AME. Collaborating with Countée had paid, I imagine, in kind. My volunteer internship amounted to 0.5 jobs. I needed a paying gig.

I became an entry-level assistant in the managing editorial department at Bantam Doubleday Dell. Which meant I did the grunt work all the other people twenty-four storeys above 666 Fifth Avenue couldn't bother doing themselves. I circulated blue-sheets and mechanicals; attended reprint and cover art meetings; took meeting minutes, typed up and distributed them; ran back and forth between the Art, Editorial, Managing Editorial and Production Departments as well as the Vice President's and Chairman's vast cool offices; evaluated and wrote reader's reports on foreign-language titles.

It paid half what I later made on Wall Street. But I learned a thing or two about the publishing rackets—how books are conceived, developed, mass-produced, marketed and remaindered.

I now had 1.5 jobs, two thirds of them paid gigs.

"Guess where," I congratulated myself, during the gourmet dinner I treated Ida Mae to with my first paycheck, "*I'm* living now."

"Not sure I wanna know, child."

"Haarlum!"

I moved to 146th Street between Convent and St. Nicholas. Reefer dens along 140th Street had given way to crack houses. Townhouses like the one I now lived in, formerly single-family units, had been chopped up into rooming houses by little old ladies from the West Indies. Every other once-elegant sandstone or brownstone on every other street was a burnt-out shell. Outside my window, I saw a car-jacking, two shootings and heard more roof-top gunplay than I could imagine in a neighborhood full of children. The homicide rate in New York City reached 1,300. Severed heads were found in garbage cans. Harlem was an abscess, scabbed over and picked at until, poisonous with pus, it burst. Harlem was a crime scene.

*

But what did that have to do with me? I was just passing through! I wasn't born addicted to drugs, and had no intention of dying from an overdose. It simply never occurred to me that the overthrow in complacent democracies of equal protection under the rule of law, basic civil liberties, and respect for the rights of the individual and for the autonomy of institutions of civil society doesn't just happen to people somewhere else who somehow may or may not deserve it, or that it could never happen here or happen to me. I was slumming.

I was now twenty-five.

In the mid-1980s, determined to make the most of what New York had to offer, many of us twenty-somethings scraped by on editorial assistant salaries. Our rent was $100 a week. We owed no back taxes, had no angry ex-wives dragging us back and forth to family court, no child support to pay. Our biggest problem in life was figuring out what to write and where to publish. And, for some of us, even that wasn't a problem because we'd become regular—paid!—contributors to *Kirkus*. For almost half a week's rent, every two weeks, we got to review any book we wanted out of the slush pile. Our kitchenettes had no kitchens. So, we hustled shopping bags full of hard-cover remainders and review copies down to the Strand Bookstore near Union Square, sold them off, then went up to Little Brazil or down to Indian restaurants on 3rd Street in the East Village, and so ate well and cheaply seven nights a week. We studied listings in *Time Out* and the About Town section of *The New Yorker*; knew every joint serving free food at happy hour; knew which day of the week every museum or other venue had free nights; knew who was giving away free tickets to see the Rangers play at Madison Square Garden, to see the Comédie-Française play Molière at the Brooklyn Academy of Music, to hear Maurizio Pollini play Carnegie Hall. In those days, nearly forty years ago, there was a different friend for every night of the week: friends for ballet, opera and other theater events; museum and art-gallery friends; friends for happy hour at Chumley's or the Lion's Head in the West Village, where Gregory Rabassa had caroused with Dylan Thomas. *The New Yorker* wasn't just some magazine we aspired to publish in. *The New Yorker* was what we lived by. Such were the days.

One of my volunteer duties was sorting and opening mail.

An annuity statement caught Ida Mae's attention.

"Don't *open* that!"

She grabbed it from my hand.

"Matter of fact, I want you to set up a meeting with Rob Bone.[3] Trusts & Estates attorney, don't you know. Have him draw up a codicil. Gonna leave you a little something in my will."

Ida Mae caught me eyeing an invitation.

"Open it, child."

In embossed gold letters, the invitation requested the honor of Ida-Cullen Cooper's presence, at a 120th anniversary event to be held at the Armory[4] at Park Avenue and 66th Street, in celebration of the countless *Nation* contributors—Du Bois, Countée, Langston, Claude McKay, Jimmy Baldwin—appearing in those pages since its founding in 1865.

She cleared the cobwebs of that notion from her mind.

I couldn't believe it.

"You aren't going?"

"Child, I am too *old* for that foolishness. You go ahead and go. One day, you'll publish in *The Nation*."

Ida Mae was in pain.

I fetched a nitroglycerine tablet.

Palms upturned, she shooed me out the door.

"Next time you come, bring me a little groceries. From Gristedes."

I left Kips Bay, headed home to Harlem, and never saw Ida Mae again.

*

On 6 May 1986, the Trust & Estates attorney handed me two things: a check worth one year's rent on a newly renovated studio with exposed-brick and hardwood-flooring, down on the fast-gentrifying Lower East Side; and a copy of the *New York Times*.

"Ida Cullen-Cooper, who spent years traveling the country to keep alive the work of her late husband, the poet Countee Cullen, died of a heart attack Saturday at her home on the East Side of Man-

---

3. The one name change I made to respect the privacy of survivors and/or living persons.

4. Wikipedia says: "The Park Avenue Armory Conservancy, generally known as Park Avenue Armory, is a nonprofit cultural institution within the historic Seventh Regiment Armory building located at 643 Park Avenue on New York City's Upper East Side. The institution displays unconventional artwork, including performing and visual arts."

hattan. She was eighty-six years old.[5] She also was active in the civic life of her neighborhood and the cultural life of Harlem, where a branch of the New York Public Library, at 104 West 136th Street near Lenox Avenue, bears the poet's name. Mr. Cullen, who died in 1946 at the age of 42, was an important writer of the Harlem Renaissance in the 1920s. Mrs. Cooper, a native of Tulsa, Oklahoma, was married to the poet in 1940. In 1953, Mrs. Cooper married Robert L. Cooper, who was widely known for his work with troubled youths. Mr. Cooper died in 1966. Survivors include a daughter, Norma Nimmons; a brother, Harry D. Roberson; a sister, Alice Mae Woods; a granddaughter, and a great-grandson."[6]

*

Countée's cotillion, a formal dinner at which Du Bois, Locke and more than one-hundred editors, agents, authors and cultural leaders were present, took place at the Civic Club. Business cards got swapped, editorial meetings scheduled. That's how Countée and Langston got their first book contracts.[7]

The Nation 120th anniversary celebration at the Armory was attended by 4,000 people. Between speeches by former presidential candidates activist Joan Baez, one of Countée's admirers, accompanied herself on guitar, and wore white silk onstage. Sidney Poitier and Langston went way back, so the man I'd seen perform *Raisin in the Sun* so many times on television offered to introduce me to Baldwin,[8] who was talking to Kurt Vonnegut.

---

5. According to Alana Teller and the Amistad Research Center at Tulane, Ida Cullen-Cooper was born on 3 January 1903—the year Countée was born—not, as the *New York Times* reports, in 1900. Ida Cullen Cooper Papers, https://amistad-finding-aids.tulane.edu/agents/people/70.

6. https://www.nytimes.com/1986/05/06/obituaries/ida-cullen-cooper-86-widow-of-harlem-renaissance-poet.html

7. http://voice-of-experience.blogspot.com/2012/03/civic-club-dinner-march-21-1924.html

8. Facts: I met Baldwin for the first time at Aaron Davis Hall, City College of New York, in 1986. Sidney Poitier was every bit as tall and gracious as he appears on film. It was he who offered to introduce me to Baldwin, not the other way around. I would never have asked him to do that, for the reasons set forth below. Anyway, Baldwin and I had subsequent phone conversations. But I no longer remember whether Baldwin and I actually talked at the Park

Jimmy odd-jobbed, during schooling and after, until he won a Rosenwald writing fellowship. When Countée's funeral took place, Jimmy, aged twenty-two, was somewhere in Greenwich Village, "writing himself," as essayist Rachel Kaadzi Ghansah says, "into the canon."[9] Two years after Richard Wright left New York, Jimmy followed in his footsteps and left for France, to what extent influenced by his middle school French teacher he seems ambivalent about admitting.

"Mr. Baldwin."

"Call me Jimmy, dammit."

In the late 1970s, I'd begun discovering his novels, plays, short stories and essay collections. Before moving to New York, I spent six months reading and writing about him, and published a long essay about his work—a piece I'd now do very differently.

"So, *you're* the one."

"I—"

"You wrote 'Alas, Poor Jimmy'."[10]

"What I meant to say—"

Abruptly, the meeting was over. I was dismissed.

*

Half a century after publication of *The Fire Next Time* (1963) I reread it side by side with Jesmyn Ward's *The Fire This Time: A New Generation Speaks about Race* (2016). An anthology of essays and poems by Claudia Rankine, Natasha Trethewey, Kevin Young and others, it reflects an entire range of emotions about race, regionalism, gender identity and American history—past, present, and future—while introducing Baldwin and many newer voices to a wider audience.

Taking cheap shots at living writers I no longer do as a reviewer. Some things I said about Baldwin in 1983 I would argue more judiciously in 2023. I would edit out received ideas about the Baldwin of *The Amen Corner* or *Blues for Mr. Charlie*, commonplaces about Bald-

---

Avenue Armory thirty-seven years ago. Because there was much alcohol and tremendous noise at that 1986 event.

9. Ward, Jesmyn, ed. *The Fire This Time: A New Generation Speaks about Race.* New York: Scribner (2016), p. 27.

10. Brown, Kevin. "The Epistles of James." *The Threepenny Review*, Vol. 19 (Autumn 1984), pp. 6–8.

win's being weakest as playwright, stronger as a writer of short fiction, but best as an essayist. It's not necessarily true that Baldwin is better at fact than fiction. That first novel Baldwin wrote in Paris, *Go Tell It on the Mountain* (1953), explores themes he revisited throughout his career: childhood; the black church; fathers and sons. On first reading, it seemed as tightly constructed and beautifully written, as deeply moving as many of his early essays.

What does seem true is that Baldwin's late nonfiction (to a less fatal degree, being relatively short) suffers, progressively, from many of the flaws that mar the late fiction—the sentimentality of *Giovanni's Room* (1956), *Another Country* (1962), *Tell Me How Long the Train's Been Gone* (1968), *If Beale Street Could Talk* (1974) and *Just Above My Head* (1980). Baldwin's talent tends toward the small effect—turns of phrase, observation of manners. Baldwin's later nonfiction relies less on rigorous argument and more on inductive insights and moral suasion. It was force of style that suasion was so dependent on. Declining craftsmanship late in Baldwin's career made fundamentally structural weaknesses glaringly apparent in his longer-form works.

Or so it struck me forty years ago. Baldwin's best work from the period after Countée's death, 1948 to 1956, is deeply personal but never self-absorbed, impassioned but not histrionic. Drawn from the life he knew intimately, it was in these books that Baldwin most succeeded in dramatizing the environment that produced him and continued to nourish him until his death. The classic essays collected in *Notes of a Native Son* (1955) contain, among others, the 10,000-word title piece, one of the great personal essays in the English language. Profound and tough, the best of these essays—"A Question of Identity," "A Stranger in the Village," "Many Thousands Gone"—consistently transcend the homiletic.

When it comes to what Carol Anderson calls White Rage, whether covert or overt in the form of mass shootings of religious worshippers and people of color, the hoods and robes have come off; it has shown its face in broad noon daylight. Given extremists' "need for human affirmation, and also for vengeance,"[11] some things Baldwin says seem as urgent now as they did when he began publishing essays seventy-five years ago.

---

11. Baldwin, James. "The Fire Next Time," from *Collected Essays of James Baldwin*. New York: Library of America (1998).

The Fire Next Time appeared in *The New Yorker* prior to being published in book form. It caused a sensation. Reviewing it, F.W. Dupee diagnosed the nature of what then seemed Baldwin's literary decline.

"*The Fire Next Time* differs," said Dupee, "in important ways from Baldwin's earlier work in the essay. Its subjects are less concrete, less clearly defined . . . he has exchanged prophecy for criticism, exhortation for analysis, and the results for his mind and style are in part disturbing."[12]

"Down at the Cross" begins as a marvelously sustained recollection of Baldwin's Harlem childhood, and provides richly detailed background to the Nation of Islam movement that sprang up in an environment so ripe for revolt. *The Fire Next Time* is vague when it comes to examining the movement itself. And the section entitled "Letter on the One Hundredth Anniversary of the Emancipation" is less an examination of the Civil Rights Movement than what Dupee calls a sermon.

Collectively, *The Fire This Time* is better at analyzing historical forces rooted in the black diaspora, forces that gave rise to the Black Lives Matter movement protests. Claudia Rankine calls the period between Ida Mae's and my birth, 1900 to 1960, "the years of passage, plantation, migration, of Jim Crow segregation, of poverty, inner cities, profiling," of entire peoples pinioned, as one poet puts it, in a carotid restraint of "poverty and history and racism."[13]

When the Dutch surrendered it to the English, there were perhaps a couple thousand blacks in New Amsterdam. During the Civil War, Harriet Tubman helped turn New York into a major stop along the Underground Railroad, swelling its black population to 15,000. By World War I, blacks in Harlem spread out from a single apartment building to occupy more than twenty-three blocks previously colonized by Germans, Jews and the Irish. Between the time Ida Mae was born and the time of her first visit there, New York's black population tripled.

---

12. Dupee, F.W. "James Baldwin and the 'Man'." *New York Review of Books* (1 February 1963). https://www.nybooks.com/articles/1963/02/01/james-baldwin-and-the-man/

13. Claudia Rankine, quoted in Jesmyn Ward, ed. *The Fire This Time: A New Generation Speaks about Race.* New York: Scribner (2016).

By the time I was born, the Great Migration saw six million sharecroppers, kitchen mechanics, skilled and unskilled laborers swarm up from rural Alabama, Florida, Georgia, Jamaica, Mississippi, North Carolina, Puerto Rico and Virginia and into urban Baltimore, Buffalo, Trenton and other cities. By the time Ida Mae turned eighteen, sixty to seventy percent of African-American men were working manufacturing jobs in places like Cleveland, where Langston graduated from high school and spent some formative years, as well as Detroit.

"Black men's feet," Zora says in *Jonah's Gourd Vine*, "learned roads. Some said good bye cheerfully . . . others fearfully, with terrors of unknown dangers in their mouths . . . others in their eagerness for distance said nothing. The daybreak found them gone. The wind said North. Trains said North. The tides and tongues said North, and men moved like the great herds before the glaciers."[14]

What Isabel Wilkerson calls socio-economic forces that made the Harlem Renaissance possible in the first place—"red-lining, over-policing, hypersegration"[15]—led to the abandonment of an underclass increasingly marginalized by inner-city flight and disinvestment on the part of middle-class blacks and other people of color.

Subways also made the Harlem Renaissance possible. Anywhere else, a photographer like James Van Der Zee wouldn't have just happened upon Marcus Garvey, in full regalia, right about the time Malcolm X was born. Though it had a large black population during the Renaissance, Harlem was not yet a slum. There were Greek coffee shops, Irish pubs, Italian fruit stands. By the time little Jimmy Baldwin entered 139, Harlem, in decline for a decade, was a ghetto. By the time my mother was born in 1940, even lower-middle-class strivers like Countée and Ida Mae were fleeing to prosperous enclaves like Tuckahoe. Black middle class flight further widened the gap between the so-called underclass and the so-called Talented Tenth. By the 1950s, Count Basie, Duke Ellington, Billie Holiday or Ella Fitzgerald were as likely to be living in Queens or on Long Island as in Harlem. Yet, at 233 people per square acre, Har-

---

14. Hurston, Zora Neale. *Jonah's Gourd Vine*. Philadelphia: J.B. Lippincott (1934), p. 232.

15. Ward, Jesmyn, ed. *The Fire This Time: A New Generation Speaks about Race*. New York: Scribner (2016), pp. 60-61.

lem's population density was surpassed only by Calcutta's. Harlem was now a slum.[16]

Was the term *Negro Problem* ever really adequate to describe the endemic crises in communities of color? Jesmyn Ward's *The Fire This Time* is a commemoration of the half-century between publication of Baldwin's book and a celebration of his successors-in-waiting. The anthology's subtitle refers to a new generation, but some contributors are in fact mid-career writers in their fifties. Claudia Rankine was born the year *The Fire Next Time* appeared. Other contributors were born during the 1970s, still others as recently as the 1980s. The proliferation from New England to Southern California of MFA and doctoral writing programs means that there are now more writers of color than ever before. Which is as it should be. Natasha Trethewey's poem "Theories of Time and Space" shares the broadly regional and specifically southern concerns of the anthology's other contributions but is otherwise notable for its very absence of an overtly racial theme. Which is as it could be.

For argument's sake but in the interest of toning down inflammatory rhetoric, let's term as foreseeable if unintended the consequences of a clash between social forces like the Great Migration and mass de-industrialization. In terms sociologist Charles S. Johnson would perhaps have called historically scientific, let's remember that there was a time when the majority of Americans of any color

---

16. It's unreasonable to expect that, just because African-Americans were oppressed by whites, they should cease to oppress each other or internalize oppression. The caste system separating "pretty niggers" like Harold Jackman from what Du Bois and many others casually referred to as the Ugliest Negroes in America (Lewis 242) is the worst-kept secret in black culture. Pauper princes and princesses of the Talented Tenth, from before-the-Mayflower families in Atlanta, Boston, Charleston, New Orleans, Philadelphia and Washington, DC, who fancied themselves the social betters of the Underclass, are routinely accused of over-relying on refined manners and proper diction to compensate for their exclusion from spheres of actual power—economic, military and political—in American life. They conversed in French, and wore gloves and bonnets to protect fair skins from the sun. Entire tomes have been written about this Afro/African-American class warfare within the color line. Maybe this is some weird, hard-wired survival-mechanism. Maybe it's much simpler. "Let's face it," Charles S. Johnson shrugged, "some Negroes are distasteful to other Negroes." Gilpin, Patrick J. "Charles S. Johnson: Entrepreneur of the Harlem Renaissance," quoted in *The Harlem Renaissance Remembered*, p. 239.

still lived on farms, producing what they consumed—shelter, food, clothing. By the tail end of the Great Migration, when I was born, most Americans had abandoned farms for cities. Many Americans then abandoned those cities for suburbs like the ones I grew up in—those who weren't redlined out of them.[17]

Sundered from self-reliance and land, marooned in urban areas where manufacturing steadily declined, producing virtually none of what they consumed, lost souls got chewed up and spit out—like wheat in a combine harvester—by mechanized ways of life. Vast Mississippi plantations got parceled into ever smaller share-cropping lots. Spacious single-family houses in Memphis, like the brownstones of Bedford-Stuyvesant, got chopped up into an urban kindling of rooming houses, and largely black male populations made-redundant by the above-mentioned socio-economic forces continue to be warehoused in forced relocation centers in numbers over-representative of their percentages of the general population.

I do remember, as vividly as if it were yesterday, Tommie Smith's and John Carlos' black power salutes, their gloved fists thrust into the flood-lit night as they refused to look up to the American flag during the national anthem at the Mexico City 1968 Summer Olympics. But I don't remember the rioting in Philadelphia, Watts, Cleveland, Omaha, Newark, Detroit, North Minneapolis, Chicago, Washington, DC or Baltimore. Perhaps because I was too young. Or perhaps because inner cities have been smoldering my entire life.

In his 1948 essay "Everybody's Protest Novel," Baldwin said of Richard Wright: "He saw clearly enough, far more clearly than I had dared allow myself to see, what I had done: I had used his work as a kind of springboard into my own. His work was a block in my road, the sphinx, really, whose riddle I had to answer before I could become myself. I thought confusedly then, and feel very definite-

---

17. In 1971 this house I lived in cost a two-income family working at the post office $57,000 in San Mateo County, California dollars. https://www.redfin.com/CA/Belmont/2736-Wemberly-Dr-94002/home/1591060. In 2023, this house cost $2,549,137. The current market value of the house Countée Cullen and my great grandmother lived in, Tuckahoe, Westchester County, 1940-1946: https://www.zillow.com/homedetails/41-Grandview-Ave-White-Plains-NY-10605/32977338_zpid/. Ida Mae probably took out a second mortgage they couldn't even have floated the first on to send my mother to boarding school at Stockbridge. https://en.wikipedia.org/wiki/Stockbridge_School.

ly now, that this was the greatest tribute I could have paid him. But it is not an easy tribute to bear, and I do not know how I will take it when my time comes."[18]

Baldwin didn't seem to be taking it very well, that night at *The Nation* 120th anniversary gala. What did I want, after all, a pat on the back? What did I hope to gain by meeting him in person?[19]

*

During the Civil Rights movement, Baldwin wrote: "I have not written about the Negro at such length because I expected that to be my only subject, but because it was the gate I had to unlock before I could hope to write about anything else."[20] Except for brief moments in *Giovanni's Room*, he never quite succeeded in unlocking that gate. But his successors can now operate from a default position other than reaction to white privilege.[21] Locke called for greater understanding and justice from the majority, but also called for less special pleading from minorities. "We wish our race pride to be a healthier, more positive achievement," Locke writes, "than a feeling based on a realization of the shortcomings of others."[22]

The year after our encounter, James Arthur Baldwin died at sixty-three—the age I turned when the book you're now reading was published. I'll say now what I should have said then. Baldwin's influence is so pervasive that, even when not directly quoted, his presence is clearly felt, whether in the work of poets like Trethewey, Young or other members of The Darkroom Collective and Cave Canem. By the nature of their relation to organized society, writers are protestors, whether as creators of archetypes or destroyers of stereotypes. They carry on, in the collective dark, struggling with hard questions.

18. Baldwin, James. "Alas, Poor Richard." *Collected Essays of James Baldwin*. New York: Library of America (1998).

19. I learned my lesson: by all means, be on intimate terms with the *work* of literary artists, performing artists and visual artists you admire; by no means does it follow you can be on good terms with their persons. Artists, at a certain age and for good reason, learn to make themselves scarce, retreat into their own work, and hobnob with colleagues and acquaintances only on rare occasions.

20. Baldwin, James. *Notes of a Native Son*. Boston. Beacon Press (1955).

21. See chapter 21 of this text at fn. 11.

22. Locke, Alain. *The New Negro*. Digital History ID 3617. https://www.digitalhistory.uh.edu/disp_textbook.cfm?smtid=3&psid=3617

Afterword

Of how he wrote the "Moloch" section of *Howl*, Allen Ginsberg said: "You have to have the right historical situation, the right physical combination, the right mental formulation, the right courage, the right sense of prophecy, and the right information."[1]

Between us we spent seventy-seven years, Ida Mae and I, living in and around New York. Without doubt, Countée would still be remembered today, even without her intervention. It's fairer to say Ida Mae Roberson's obituary wouldn't have been news fit to print in the paper of record if not for her marriage to Countée Cullen. Regardless, I owe my very existence to her as a matter of biological fact. And I can't imagine sustaining a literary life—lived well, lived wisely, grounded in material reality—without the example of their life together. We remain—Countée, Ida Mae and I, in some cases by blood, in other cases by marriage but in each case by a sense of shared history and tradition—a family, inseparable.

Sometimes, I felt Ida Mae was grooming me to take over the family business. One of the many gifts she imparted was a sense of the relative ordinariness—banality, even—of literary life. By bringing me into contact with older, established writers, she gave me a glimpse of what it means to belong to an artistic community, to run the great risks and reap the commensurately unremunerative rewards of literary life. To this day, even in my solitude I never feel I'm working in isolation—marginalized, unsupported, misunderstood. My predecessors number in the thousands. Of my contemporaries I can't even keep count.

Other times, naturally, I did feel Ida Mae was stifling rather than nurturing my ambitions as a writer. More than once, she hinted I might end up writing about Countée. In my terrible twenties, I simply had no idea how rich the material for this group portrait might be. Rolled my eyes in contempt; suspected myself of being manipulated into running what amounted to literary errands, like fetching groceries from Gristedes or messengering copy jobs over to Kinko's. I had my own biography to live, my own books to write.

---

1. Schumacher, *Dharma Lion*, p. 204.

I see our relationship followed an old pattern. Clashes arose between Old Guardians and Young Turks. Ida Mae was among the last of the Old Guardians. I was just another Young Turk. Like any Young Turk, I'm still hell bent on following my agenda. Occasionally I consent to be of use—up to a point—as a means to greater movements' ends. In our case, it just so happened my ambition coincided with Ida Mae's diminished appetite for official duties, though not for power.

I never imagined during Ida Mae's lifetime—any more than she imagined she'd travel the world reading Countée's work and lecturing about him after his sudden death—that I'd end up writing about her. I underestimated Ida Mae, as both ally and opponent. Had no clue how successfully she'd scheme to make me invest this many years of life on a subject I swore I had no interest in. Don't put it past her to have masterminded this entire operation in the first place.

Now I'm ready.

Chronology

1886   James Van Der Zee born June 29

1887   Sargent Claude Johnson born October 7

1890   Palmer Hayden born January 15

1890   James Van Der Zee born June 29

1891   Archibald J. Motley, Jr. born October 7

1892   Augusta Savage born February 29

1896   Malvin Gray Johnson born January 28

1900   Hale Aspacio Woodruff born August 26

1901   Richmond Barthé born January 28
        William H. Johnson born March 18

1903   January 3, born: Ida Mae Roberson in Tulsa, OK
        May 30, born: Countee Leroy Porter in [Louisville, KY?]

1905   Lois Mailou Jones born November 3

1907   Charles H. Alston born November 28

1909   National Association for the Advancement of Colored People founded

1914   World War I begins
        Claude McKay arrives in Harlem

1915   Booker T. Washington dies
        Alfred A. Knopf founds Borzoi Books; H.L. Mencken and Carl Van Vechten are among its first authors

1916   The Great Migration begins
        James Van Der Zee opens photography studio in Harlem

1917   United States enters World War I
        370,000 African-Americans perform military service
        Race riots occur in East St. Louis, Illinois
        Thousands of African-Americans march in silent protest down Fifth Avenue in New York City
        Alain Locke publishes his dissertation, *Race Contacts and Inter-Racial Relationships*
        Claude McKay publishes poems in *Seven Arts*

1918   World War I ends

1919   Claude McKay publishes protest poem "If We Must Die" in
        The Liberator
        New York City hosts a homecoming parade honoring mem-
        bers of the all-black 369th Infantry Regiment for valor
        during World War I
        From April to October upwards of 1,000 blacks and whites
        are killed, injured or made homeless during riots that
        erupt nationwide during the "Red Summer"
        Marcus Garvey founds the Black Star Line

1920   Palmer Hayden studies at Cooper Union

1921   William H. Johnson enrolls in the National Academy
        of Design

1922   Countée Cullen graduates from DeWitt Clinton, a public
        preparatory school

1923   *Opportunity*, the magazine of the Urban League, is
        first published

1924   Aaron Douglas moves to New York City, begins studying
        with Winold Reiss; E.M. Forster's *Passage to India* appears;
        Virginia Woolf delivers a lecture at Cambridge University,
        "Mr. Bennet and Mrs. Brown."

1926   Harmon Foundation holds first annual competition
        and exhibition of artwork submitted for "Distinguished
        Achievement Among Negroes"

1929   Stock market crash

1930   Lois Mailou Jones accepts teaching post at How-
        ard University

1931   Hale Woodruff accepts teaching post at Atlanta University

1933   President Franklin Delano Roosevelt takes office

1934   Malvin Gray Johnson dies October 4

1935   Last Harmon Foundation competition held
        Works Progress Administration (WPA) begins

1937   Harlem Community Art Center opens, managed by
Augusta Savage
Claude McKay publishes *A Long Way from Home*
Henry Ossawa Tanner dies in Paris

1939   American ship is sunk in the Atlantic, preventing Countée
Cullen from traveling back and forth to Europe
Aaron Douglas begins teaching at Fisk University

1940   World War II begins in Europe

1945   World War II ends

1947   William H. Johnson committed to Central Islip State Hospital 1948

1960   Kevin Brown born in Kansas City, Missouri, 3 September

1962   Augusta Savage dies on March 27

1963   W.E.B. Du Bois dies

1967   Sargent Claude Johnson dies

1969   "Harlem On My Mind" art exhibition opens at the Metropolitan Museum of Art

1970   William H. Johnson dies

1973   Arna Bontemps dies on June 4
Palmer Hayden dies

1979   Aaron Douglas dies

1980   President Jimmy Carter honors ten African-American artists at the White House

1981   Archibald J. Motley dies

1983   James Van Der Zee dies

1986   Ida Cullen-Cooper dies in New York City on May 3

1988   Romare Bearden dies

1989   Richmond Barthé dies on March 5

Select Bibliography

Anderson, Jervis. *This Was Harlem: A Cultural Portrait, 1900–1950.* Farrar, Straus & Giroux, 1982.

Aptheker, Herbert. *Correspondence of W.E.B. Du Bois, Vol. 1, Selections: 1877–1934.* University of Massachusetts Press, 1973.

Bernard, Emily. *Remember Me to Harlem: The Letters of Langston Hughes and Carl Van Vechten.* Alfred A. Knopf, 2001.

—. Bernard, Emily. *Carl Van Vechten and the Harlem Renaissance: A Portrait in Black and White.* Yale University Press, 2012.

Bontemps, Arna. *Harlem Renaissance Remembered.* Dodd, Mead & Co., 1972.

Boyd, Valerie. *Wrapped in Rainbows: The Life of Zora Neale Hurston.* Scribner, 2003

Schmidt-Campbell, Mary. *Harlem Renaissance: Art of Black America.* Abrams, 1987.

—. *An American Odyssey: The Life and Work of Romare Bearden.* Oxford University Press, 2018.

Charters, Ann. *Portable Beat Reader.* Viking, 1992.

Cooper, Wayne F. *Claude McKay, Rebel Sojourner in the Harlem Renaissance: A Biography.* Louisiana State University Press, 1987.

Cullen, Countée. *The Black Christ and Other Poems.* Harper & Brothers, 1929.

—. *Caroling Dusk: An Anthology of Verse by Black Poets.* 1927. Carol Publishing Group, 1993.

—. *Color.* Harper & Brothers, 1925.

—. *Lost Zoo.* 1940. The Silver Burdett Press, 1992.

—. *The Medea and Some Poems.* Harper & Brothers, 1935.

—. *My Lives and How I Lost Them.* Harper & Brothers, 1942.

—. *One Way to Heaven.* Harper and Brothers, 1932.

—. *On These I Stand: The Best Poems of Countée Cullen.* Harper & Brothers, 1947.

Dancy, John. *Sand Against the Wind.* Wayne State University Press, 1966.

Davis, Arthur, and Michael Peplow, eds. *New Negro Renaissance: An Anthology.* Holt, Rinehart & Winston, 1975.

Douglas, Ann. *Terrible Honesty: Mongrel Manhattan in the 1920s.* Farrar, Straus & Giroux, 1995.

Du Bois, W. E. B. *Souls of Black Folk.* 1903. Fawcett, 1961.

Early, Gerald, ed. *My Soul's High Song: The Collected Writings of Countée Cullen, Voice of the Harlem Renaissance.* Doubleday, 1991.

Hatch, James V. *Sorrow Is the Only Faithful One: The Life of Owen Dodson.* University of Illinois Press, 1993.

Hemenway, Robert. *Zora Neale Hurston: A Literary Biography.* University of Illinois Press, 1977.

Huggins, Nathan Irvin. *Harlem Renaissance.* Oxford University Press, 1971.

Huggins, Nathan Irvin. *Voices from the Harlem Renaissance.* Oxford University Press, 1995.

Hughes, Langston. *The Big Sea.* Alfred A. Knopf, 1940.

—. *The Collected Poems of Langston Hughes.* Edited by Arnold Rampersad. Penguin Random House, 1994.

Hurston, Zora Neale. *Dust Tracks on a Road.* J.P. Lippincott, 1942.

Hutchinson, George. *The Harlem Renaissance in Black and White.* Belknap Press of Harvard University Press, 1997.

"Ida Cullen Cooper, 86, Widow of Harlem Renaissance Poet." *NY Times,* 6 May 1986.

Jackson, Major, ed. *Countée Cullen: Collected Poems.* Library of America, 2013.

Johnson, James Weldon. *Along This Way.* 1993. Da Capo Press, 2000.

—. *Autobiography of an Ex-Coloured Man.* 1912. Penguin Random House, 1990.

—. *Black Manhattan.* 1930. Da Capo Press, 1991.

—. *Book of American Negro Poetry.* 1922. Harcourt Brace, 1959.

Kaplan, Carla, ed. *Zora Neale Hurston: A Life in Letters.* Doubleday, 2002.

—. *Miss Annie in Harlem: The White Women of the Harlem Renaissance.* HarperCollins, 2013.

Keats, John. *Poems.* 1944. Everyman's Library/Knopf, 1992.

—. *Selected Letters.* Penguin Classics, 2015.

Kellner, Bruce, ed. *Harlem Renaissance: A Historical Dictionary of the Era.* Greenwood Press, 1984.

Kerman, Cynthia Earl. *The Lives of Jean Toomer: A Hunger for Wholeness.* Louisiana State University Press, 1987.

Kisselhoff, Jeff. *You Must Remember This: An Oral History of Manhattan from the 1890s to World War II.* Harcourt Brace Jovanovich, 1989.

Lewis, David Levering. *The Portable Harlem Renaissance Reader.* Viking, 1994.

—. *When Harlem Was in Vogue.* 1981. Knopf/Penguin, 1997.

—. *W. E. B. Du Bois, 1868–1919: Biography of a Race.* Henry Holt, 1993.

—. *W. E. B. Du Bois, 1919–1963: The Fight for Equality and the American Century.* Henry Holt, 2000.

—. *Voices from the Renaissance.* Interviews. Special Collections, Schomburg Center for Research in Black culture, New York Public Library, n.p. n.d.

Locke, Alain, ed. *The New Negro: Voices of the Harlem Renaissance.* 1925. Touchstone, 1999.

McKay, Cladius Festus. *A Long Way from Home.* 1937. Rutgers University Press, 2007.

Molesworth, Charles. *And Bid Him Sing: A Biography of Countée Cullen.* University of Chicago Press, 2012.

Molesworth, Charles (with Leonard Harris). *Alain L. Locke: The Biography of a Philosopher.* University of Chicago Press, 2008.

Nichols, Charles H., ed. *Arna Bontemps–Langston Hughes Letters, 1925–1967.* Dodd, Mead, 1980.

Pinckney, Darryl. "The Sweet Singer of Tuckahoe." *New York Review of Books* 5 March 1992.

Rampersad, Arnold. *The Life of Langston Hughes Vol. 1, 1902–1941: I, Too, Sing America.* Oxford University Press, 1986.

—. *The Life of Langston Hughes Vol. 2, 1941–1967: I Dream a World.* Oxford University Press, 1988.

Rampersad, Arnold, David Roessel, and Christa Fratantoro, eds. *The Selected Letters of Langston Hughes.* Alfred A. Knopf, 2015.

Redding, Jay Saunders. *To Make a Poet Black.* University of North Carolina Press, 1939.

Schoener, Allen, ed. *Harlem on My Mind: 1900–1968.* Random House, 1969.

Sing, Amrijit; Scott, Daniel M. III. *The Collected Writings of Wallace Thurman: A Harlem Renaissance Reader.* Rutgers University Press, 2003.

Stewart, Jeffrey C. *The New Negro: The Life of Alain Locke.* Oxford University Press, 2018.

Taylor, Yuval. *Zora and Langston: A Story of Friendship and Betrayal.* W.W. Norton, 2019.

Thurman, Wallace. *Infants of the Spring.* Macaulay Co., 1932.

—. *Negro Life in New York's Harlem.* Haldeman-Julius Publications, 1928.

Toomer, Jean. *Cane.* 1923. Horace Liveright, 1975.

Watson, Steven. *Birth of the Beat Generation: Visionaries, Rebels, and Hipsters, 1944–1960.* Pantheon, 1988.

—. *The Harlem Renaissance: Hub of African-American Culture, 1920–1930.* Pantheon, 1995.

—. *Strange Bedfellows: The First American Avant-Garde.* Abbeville Press, 1991.

West, Dorothy. *Where the Wild Grape Grows: Selected Writings, 1930–1950.* University of Massachusetts Press, 2005.

White, Edward. *The Tastemaker: Carl Van Vechten and the Birth of Modern America.* Farrar, Straus & Giroux, 2014.

Wilkerson, Isabel. *The Warmth of Other Suns: The Epic Story of America's Great Migration.* Random House, 2010.

Wintz, Cary D., and Paul Finkelman. *Encyclopedia of the Harlem Renaissance.* Routledge, 2004.

Credits

Grateful acknowledgment is made to the following for permission to reprint previously published and unpublished material:

Amistad Research Center, Tulane

John L. Dennis Revocable Trust (Selections from *The Collected Poems of Sterling A. Brown*, selected by Michael S. Harper. Copyright© 1980 by Sterling A. Brown. Reprinted by permission of the John L. Dennis Revocable Trust.)

Community Oral History Project, New York Public Library.

Harold Ober Associates Incorporated: Excerpts from letters from Langston Hughes to various correspondents. Published in *Life of Langston Hughes* by Arnold Rampersad (New York: Oxford University Press, ©1986, 1988 by Arnold Rampersad). Reprinted by permission.

Howard University: Excerpts from the letters of Alain Locke. Alain Locke Papers, Moorland-Spingarn Research Center, Howard University. Reprinted by permission.

"The Seine, c. 1902" by Henry Ossawa Tanner. Oil on canvas. Gift of Henry Tanner Moore to the Avalon Foundation. Courtesy of the National Gallery of Art Collection. Public domain.

The New York Public Library: Excerpts from "Voices of the Renaissance," interviews by David Levering Lewis. David L. Lewis "Voices of the Renaissance" Collection, Manuscripts, Archives and Rare Books Division, Schomburg Center for Research in Black Culture, The New York Public Library. Reprinted by permission.

Schomburg Center for Research in Black culture at the New York Public Library, Special Collections.

Yale University: James Weldon Johnson Collection, Yale Collection of American Literature, Beinecke Rare Book and Manuscript Library, Yale University. Reprinted by permission.

About the Author

Author, essayist, literary translator and reviewer Kevin Anthony Brown was born 3 September 1960, in Kansas City, Missouri. He earned his Bachelor's degree from the City University of New York. Kevin A. Brown is a member of the National Book Critics Circle. He currently lives in San Diego.

Self-portrait. © 2020.

Index

Printed in the USA
CPSIA information can be obtained
at www.ICGtesting.com
CBHW030213220724
11829CB00002B/7

9 781643 174273